RUSSIAN TRANSPORT

BY ERIKA SHEFFER

★

★

DRAMATISTS
PLAY SERVICE
INC.

SPECIAL NOTE

Anyone receiving permission to produce RUSSIAN TRANSPORT is required to give credit to the Author as sole and exclusive Author of the Play on the title page of all programs distributed in connection with performances of the Play and in all instances in which the title of the Play appears for purposes of advertising, publicizing or otherwise exploiting the Play and/or a production thereof. The name of the Author must appear on a separate line, in which no other name appears, immediately beneath the title and in size of type equal to 50% of the size of the largest, most prominent letter used for the title of the Play. No person, firm or entity may receive credit larger or more prominent than that accorded the Author. The following acknowledgment must appear on the title page in all programs distributed in connection with performances of the Play:

Originally produced in New York City by The New Group (Scott Elliott, Artistic Director).

SPECIAL NOTE ON SONGS AND RECORDINGS

For performances of copyrighted songs, arrangements or recordings mentioned in this Play, the permission of the copyright owner(s) must be obtained. Other songs, arrangements or recordings may be substituted provided permission from the copyright owner(s) of such songs, arrangements or recordings is obtained; or songs, arrangements or recordings in the public domain may be substituted.

For my father, Yuri Sheffer

RUSSIAN TRANSPORT was presented by the New Group (Scott Elliott, Artistic Director; Geoff Rich, Executive Director) in New York City, opening on January 30, 2012. It was directed by Scott Elliott; the set design was by Derek McLane; the costume design was by Ann Hould-Ward; the lighting design was by Peter Kaczorowski; the sound design was by Bart Fasbender; the dialect coach was Doug Paulson; the fight director was David Anzuelo; the assistant director was Marie Masters; the production supervisor was Peter R. Feuchtwanger/PRF Productions; and the production stage manager was Valerie A. Peterson. The cast was as follows:

DIANA .... Janeane Garofalo
MISHA .... Daniel Oreskes
BORIS .... Morgan Spector
MIRA .... Sarah Steele
ALEX .... Raviv Ullman

Russian translations and coaching provided by Vera Berlyavsky.

CHARACTERS

ALEX — 18, a senior in high school.

MIRA — 14, Alex's sister, a freshman in high school.

MISHA — Father to Mira and Alex. Russian immigrant.

DIANA — Mother to Mira and Alex. Russian immigrant.

BORIS — Diana's brother. Russian immigrant.

SONYA, VERA, SVETA — Three different Russian teenagers, played by the actress playing Mira.

PLACE

Sheepshead Bay, Brooklyn.

TIME

The present.

THE SCRIPT

When words have hyphens between them (I-mean-for-your-GPA-You know-what's-GPA?), a quick change of thought is indicated.

Sometimes this is used in indicating the rhythm, as well.

A slash (/) indicates overlapping dialogue.

A dash (—) indicates an interruption or quick cue pickup.

English translations immediately follow Russian dialogue.

SET AND LIGHTS

The play is set in a house; however, there is room for an expressionist or poetic interpretation. The lines blur. The car scenes should be staged theatrically, with minimal additional scenery. Lighting, actor placement and the audience's imagination ought to do the work.

A NOTE ON THIS FAMILY

This is a family of noise. With the exception of Boris, they most often speak before they think. They are not measured in their anger, fear, humor or passion.

RUSSIAN TRANSPORT

ACT ONE

Scene 1

The house. Stage right we see the office of the car service. There is a door that leads offstage to the dispatch booth downstairs, and a street exit. Another door connects to the living/dining room area, which occupies stage left. There is an exit to an offstage kitchen, and another to the street. A staircase leads upstairs, where we see Mira's bedroom. A song like Vladimir Visotsky's "My Gypsy Song" plays as an air mattress inflates within a cabinet in the wall unit.* The cabinet doors are pushed open. The bed blows up. It rests in a downstage corner. Lights bump up. Mira sits at the table.

MIRA. *(Calling upstairs.)* And-it's-like-a-cross-cultural-thing? It's like you learn about other cultures — About broadening-like-expanding-your experiences and stuff! Ma! *(No answer.)* Ma, it's like really good for college applications, but also for your world-view! I mean for your GPA-You-know-what's-GPA? It's grade-point average. *(Diana enters with two full garbage bags and unpacks clothes into a cabinet.)*
DIANA. It's expensive, no?
MIRA. I-guess-but-I-mean-they-got-scholarships.
DIANA. Uh-hah —
MIRA. And the one I applied for is in Florence.
DIANA. It's the worst anti-Semites in Florence. Only in Arab countries is worse.

MIRA. That's bullshit —

DIANA. / Shht!

MIRA. The shortest one is only four weeks, which is nothing, which is like half of break —

DIANA. You gonna be away from all you friends.

MIRA. Who? Ilona?

DIANA. Don't say like Ilona like you better, like you special.

MIRA. I'm not.

DIANA. You not —

MIRA. Arright, I know. Hey-is-that-my-sweatpants? Whatayou doing?

DIANA. You sleeping on za air mattress, now.

MIRA. What? Nuh-uh! *(Diana continues unpacking.)* I'm not sleeping down here —

DIANA. Shut-tup —

MIRA. Why can't he sleep on / the —

DIANA. Shut-tup.

MIRA. Greesha slept on the air mattress when he came. I'm not giving up my room.

DIANA. Is different with Boris.

MIRA. Why —

DIANA. Because-I'm-telling-you-so-shut-you-mouth.

MIRA. If you, like, give me a reason, instead of just talking to me like I'm RETARDED, maybe I wouldn't —

DIANA. Listen to me.

MIRA. What?

DIANA. From now on you take you clothes into the bathroom when you shower, you understand?

MIRA. You're so gross.

DIANA. And wear a bra.

MIRA. I don't need to.

DIANA. You need to! I'm looking at you right now. You like a gorilla, swinging from tree to tree. *(She tosses an alarm clock on the mattress.)* Travel alarm, it got the Indiglo lights.

MIRA. This is bullshit.

DIANA. I told you watch your mouth? I told you —

MIRA. Oh my God, I hate you.

DIANA. Tell me again. In my face, tell me.

MIRA. *(Looking her in the face.)* I hate you —

DIANA. Aie, you sucha bitch —

MIRA. If I'm such a bitch, why can't I go just away this summer? Why you wanna bitch in the house, anyway?

DIANA. For fun. *(Mira receives a text message.)*

MIRA. You can't just kick me out of my own room, you know.

DIANA. Listen, if I want your kidney, I take it. If I want blood from you body, it's mine —

MIRA. Okay, that's like full-on abuse —

DIANA. You skull? I gonna crush it like a nectarine — Check-za — texting-arready! *(Mira looks at her phone.)*

MIRA. Coney Island Avenue.

DIANA. By where?!

MIRA. I don't know.

DIANA. Call Alex, please — He should be home arready.

MIRA. Whatayou, Helen Keller?

DIANA. Ungrateful. You are very ungrateful girl. Call you brother.

MIRA. *(Dialing.)* Greesha slept down here when he came — It's-not-fair.

DIANA. Fair? Your grandmother was raped by Nazis. This is fair, this life? Well?

MIRA. It's ringing. *(In the distance, there is the sound of a dog barking. Alex enters the office, and the barking gets louder.)*

ALEX. Arright, arright, I'm here!

DIANA. Slava Bogu! *[Thank God!]*

MIRA. What is that?

ALEX. It's a dog.

MIRA. Why you got a dog barking for your ringer?

ALEX. It's only for when *you* call.

MIRA. Why?

ALEX. Figure it out.

DIANA. Hey, you bring something? Wine-flower-cake-nothing?

ALEX. Whadayou want-I'll-get it right now.

DIANA. I don' wanna thing — What-should I want?

ALEX. So lee me alone, arready — Jesus!

DIANA. Mira, go take the pot off the stove, please — The *pilmenye [ravioli]* gonna be too soft. *(No answer.)* Mira. *(To Alex.)* Ach, give me a minute. *(Diana exits to the kitchen.)*

ALEX. What's wrong with you? … Are you gonna cry?

MIRA. No.

ALEX. Good. It smells when you cry.

MIRA. No it doesn't —

9

ALEX. I'm so fuckin' hungry, I'm running here like it's ridiculous. Jesus, you know what I had today? School, Store, Car Service, back to Verizon. And I had like a fucking smoothie — that's it. A whole day, and that's it?

MIRA. My phone's not taking the charge.

ALEX. Yeah? You took the battery out and force a restart?

MIRA. Yeah, it's not taking. *(As Alex resets the phone.)* I told you I did that already.

DIANA. *(Reentering.)* Oh, you're talking / now? —

ALEX. You're overcharging it —

DIANA. *(To Alex.)* Take your shoes off!

MIRA. I'm not / overcharging —

DIANA. No respect for the carpet. Nobody has respect for the carpet.

ALEX. I bet you fifty bucks. You did it with the last one. What, you plug it in at night? Until you wake up, it's like seven hours. It's too long. I told you it's too long, and now you fuckin' breakin' another one, again?

MIRA. I'm not / I swear —

ALEX. I can't like guarantee you anything. It's not under the warranty. *(To Diana.)* You know where they at / or what?

DIANA. What, you have somewhere to be?

ALEX. Maybe.

DIANA. Maybe? What's this, maybe?

ALEX. Nothing, I —

DIANA. What?

ALEX. You don' have to know all my business.

DIANA. Oh-ho, now he got business?

ALEX. No, I / just —

DIANA. You got stock and bond for business? Hah? I can buy stock from you, I c'buy bond?

ALEX. Yeah, I'm going public.

DIANA. Mira, get the vinegar. *(Mira ignores her.)* I'm very sorry Mira — Please get the vinegar — I'm very sorry —

MIRA. Arright look — I'll sleep down here, but only for tonight.

DIANA. Okay-Thank-you-You-a-good-girl.

MIRA. I'm not doing this for you —

DIANA. Okay —

MIRA. It's for Boris.

MIRA. So he feels valued, or / whatever —

DIANA. Good girl. *(Mira exits.)*

10

ALEX. What's with her —

DIANA. Who-the-fuck-knows. *(She reaches on top of the wall unit and pulls down a manila envelope, as he gives her cash from his wallet. She counts it out.)* You stop by dispatch just now? You see some drivers, or what?

ALEX. You don't gotta always be checking up on them.

DIANA. Alex. They steal. This is everything?

ALEX. You-know-it's-like, someone calls, they get on the radio and send a car out. Even if I'm not there, the tree still fuckin' fell in the forest ... You know, like how if a tree falls in the forest —

DIANA. What you think only the government is stealing you money? No, no, no. You know what Lenin is saying and what Trotsky is saying? In capitalism the workers is stealing from you also. Because they Jealous for the owners. This is everything? Car service and Verizon?

ALEX. I told you, yes. It's gonna cover this month or what? *(She makes an "I don't know" gesture.)*

DIANA. Hey, lemme ask you stupid question-just-like-putting-za-bug in-za-bee. You think what you gonna say to you uncle, tonight?

ALEX. Why I gotta practice? Maybe he should practice what he's gonna say to me.

DIANA. I'm gonna skin you alive —

ALEX. Seriously, he's the one just getting here — Like, maybe he gonna need me to get *him* a job. I'm the one who's got like — Who's like connected or whatever.

DIANA. Where you "connecting"?

ALEX. Just like — At Verizon.

DIANA. Hey. At Verizon?

ALEX. Yeah ... Yes! *(Mira reenters with Swiss Fudge Stella d'Oro cookies.)*

MIRA. Alex: How old do you think someone should be before they can get on an airplane alone?

DIANA. You better put za fucking cookies away —

MIRA. Fourteen is old. There's kids whose parents get divorced, who fly when they're five —

DIANA. Shhh! ... I hear the garage door. *(To Alex.)* You hear?

ALEX. I'm not a fucking coyote.

DIANA. Get za booze. *(Mira gets shot glasses. Alex pulls out bottles from the liquor cabinet.)* Amaretto, also. *(The door bursts open. Misha barrels in, all bull in china shop, followed by Boris, who brings luggage. The commotion of greeting.)*

11

MISHA. Maya syemya, mayo bogatstva! *[My family, my treasure!]* Maya dautchka. Eta Mira. Crassivaya, da? Ne mnojka prishey, no tolka na l-boo. *[My daughter. This is Mira. Beautiful, no? Some acne, but only mild, only on the forehead.]* I tell him you got zit, you got pimple! But not so bad — It go away before you wedding day — Before you wedding day, it go away!

MIRA. Pop —

BORIS. Hey, look at you big girl! She looking different from pictures, on za computer.

DIANA. Boris. Boris. Tvoyo litzaw. Paglyadee na cvoyo litzaw. *[Your face. Look at your face.]* He is, you uncle is virile man.

BORIS. Diana —

DIANA. Even he was young, everyone know. Boris Fodorovsky makes the girls pregnant only from looking. Always, he is like this. Mi ochen starry. Pasmatree na moi rukye. *[We're so old. Look at my hands.]* Liver spot! In America everything, it has a name. So you can talk about how it make you feel. Always you talk about how you are feeling. Vse govyaniye hydozjnyekie. *[Everyone's a bullshit artist.]*

MISHA. Ladno, ladno. On golodniy. *[Okay, okay. He's hungry.]* Fucking Wan Wyck-Fucking-Wan-Wyck-Expressway! Bumper ee bumper! *[Bumper and bumper.]*

DIANA. *(To Boris.)* Ya hachoo na tebya posmotret. Ti pomnyesh kak mi plavolee V"Tereke? Nyet, on ne pomnyet. *[I want to look at you. Do you remember swimming in the Terek with me? No, he doesn't remember.]* *(To Mira and Alex.)* When I see him last time? When I was seeing him — I was big sister! Now you see how tall? He never gonna stop growing.

MISHA. Big-you-still-big-Only-you bigger sideways!

DIANA. Shut-tup!

MISHA. You bigger like bottom of snowman, I'm right?

DIANA. Shut-tup arready, I'm telling you! Alex, you don't say hello to you uncle?

ALEX. Hey, how ya' doin'?

DIANA. What this "Hey"? Come-on.

BORIS. On ogromniy — Kak kaltooriste. *[He's big, yeah — Like a bodybuilder.]*

ALEX. / Uh —

BORIS. You, eh — You big guy now.

ALEX. Oh, thanks.

BORIS. You speaking Russian, you remembering?

MISHA. Ach, why he need zis?

ALEX. For sure.

DIANA. He speak-Also-understanding. Almost everything believe me —

MISHA. Better you forget, please —

DIANA. You crazy —

MISHA. What? Only two things is important you know how to say in Russian. Number one: How much zis cost? Number two: Please let go of my arm.

BORIS. Gledee na etava parnya. *[Look at this guy.]* You remember last time you see me?

ALEX. No way, man. I was what, like three —

BORIS. "No way man." Wow, he sounding just like a movie.

DIANA. Kanyeshna. *[Of course.]* Come on, you very hungry, no?

BORIS. Little bit, I uh —

DIANA. We have to feed him or he gonna send on email to everyone back home — I come to New York — nobody give me nothing to eat.

MISHA. So we eat-Who-za-fuck is stopping you?

DIANA. Snemee obuv, pazjalasta. *[Shoes off, please.]* Go sit you feet. Mira, come help me with the pilmenye.

MIRA. What's so hard about it?

MISHA. Help you mother — She-is-arthritis. She is old like dead-body — Her-bones-is gonna snap when she picks up za pot.

MIRA. Good. *(Diana and Mira exit to the kitchen. Misha, Boris and Alex settle on the couch.)*

MISHA. You sleeping on za plane, or what?

BORIS. Little bit, you know, but God, it was taking me four hours just in za airport in Moscow.

MISHA. / Shtaw? *[What?]*

BORIS. Yeah, is crazy now, since they having all za —

MISHA. Ah / okay —

BORIS. All za bombs. Listen, I was going through security, they have now little dog everywhere — Smelling you up, like you a piece of meat. One come up to me, this big — He smelling my bag maybe ten minutes, and za guy — his, you know —

MISHA. Za owner —

BORIS. I don' he own him, but yeah, he looking at me too, up and down, and he say za dog smell something.

ALEX. Shit.

BORIS. Yeah. I'm thinking, I don' have nothing — Shtaw? Ya idiotka? *[What am I, an idiot?]* So, I ask him — What you mean? He tell me, za dog smelling five hundred rubles in my bag.

MISHA. Oy, God, lotta shit — Lotta / shit!

BORIS. Yeah, for sure … Zis one, I can' believe. Mama telling me you working wiz mobile phone.

ALEX. Uh-huh.

BORIS. Is very good, technology. Important for world economics.

MISHA. World economics —

ALEX. It's decent.

MISHA. Selling phones to za blacks? Sure, he like saving za economy —

ALEX. Whatever.

MISHA. *(To Alex.)* Listen to me, Alex. Za phones / Is bullshit.

ALEX. Is bullshit.

MISHA. What I'm telling you? You spend too much time in za cell phone. Too much time on Flatbush Avenue.

ALEX. Fish gotta swim, yo' —

MISHA. They gonna shoot you one day you working there. Bop! Steal you money — Steal you iPhone. Bop-bop-bop! Is very dangerous place.

ALEX. You only ever drive through it.

MISHA. Alex, I'm reading Cop Shot in the *Post*! Always with the guns in Flatbush Brownsville. Is bad place. Anyway, you gotta be more in car service in dispatch in za books of za business.

BORIS. Ah, you are taking over Poppa work?

ALEX. I'm not sure / yet —

MISHA. Of course-No-question. *(Misha drinks.)* Ti koopeal duty free? *[You get Duty Free?]* Vodky mozhet b'eat? *[Maybe vodka?]*

BORIS. Kanyeshna. *[Of course.]*

ALEX. *(To Boris.)* So, you know like what you're gonna be doing or what?

MISHA. Slavo Bogoo. *[Thank God.]*

BORIS. Doing like whatchu mean?

ALEX. I mean for a job.

BORIS. Eh, you know, I got some like — Prospect.

MISHA. Prospect.

BORIS. Yeah.

ALEX. Well, I mean if you want, I could ask at the store — See if they got somethin'.

14

BORIS. Sure, sound / good —

MISHA. No, no, no come on. He not working in za cell phone wiz you.

ALEX. Whatever, it's somethin'. Maybe part / time —

MISHA. Ti dolzjen koopeat *New York Times* classified section, da? *[You have to get* New York Times *classified section, no?]* Tell me, they selling *New York Times* by za deli? *(To Boris.)* Listen, here you can make good work — Clean work, you know what I'm saying?

BORIS. Yeah, I know — Spaceba. *[Thanks.]*

MISHA. They selling it over there, or what?

ALEX. Nobody finds jobs like that anymore.

MISHA. What you talking?

ALEX. It's all online — Like if you don' know someone you gotta go online.

MISHA. Yeah? Is on Internet?

ALEX. Yeah.

MISHA. Everything is on Internet, now — I'm telling you. Clothes-books-a-wife. This is how is working now for young guy, no?

ALEX. I guess —

MISHA. When you want a little something — You know like little ... *(Misha makes an obscene gesture.)*

ALEX. Pop —

MISHA. Okay, okay — But this what you doing right? A log on.

ALEX. Arright. I don't need to find girls online. I don't! I gotta like, pull 'em off my dick before I go to work.

MISHA. *(Laughter.)* Hew, hew! He gotta pull them off! Is true, is true. The girls, they wanna catch you. He gotta pull 'em off. *(To Boris.)* You also gotta pull 'em off, no?

BORIS. I don't know if —

MISHA. You got a girl back home?

BORIS. Come on. Ya rabocheey, nye romanteek. Ya chlyen prolateriata. *[I am a worker, not a romantic. I am a member of the proletariat.]*

MISHA. He is proletariat, not a romantic, he telling me —

ALEX. I got it.

MISHA. Ti nye romanteek. Ya tebya znayoo. *[You are not a romantic. I know you.]* I'm not stupid. I know what you are. *(A small silence. Mira and Diana enter with steaming dishes.)*

DIANA. Okay, everybody hungry, hungry, no? Nu, come on! Sit around. Harosho, oo nas yeste conyak, yeste amaretta, yeste kaluah, yeste vwodka. Oo nas yeste peevo? *[Good, we have cognac, we have amaretto, we have Kahlua, we have vodka. We have beer?]* Mira, there is beer in the fridge?

MIRA. I dunno.

ALEX. I'll go.

MISHA. Yeah, also put on za apron wiz za ruffle!

ALEX. Why you gotta bust me —

MISHA. I'm busting? So give me a kick, I'm busting! *(To Boris.)* No, no — He a good boy. Arready he gotta shave, what? Once a week wiz a razor? Ping-ping-ping.

DIANA. Okay, no beer. We use it up, arready. So, sit. Sadyeec, pazjalasta. *[Sit, please.]* Cognac?

MISHA. Vwodkoo! *[Vodka!]*

DIANA. Boris?

BORIS. Cognac, pazjalasta. *[Cognac, please.]*

ALEX. Cognac. Yeah, me too.

DIANA. Mira, watchu want?

MIRA. Nothing.

DIANA. Okay so a little vodka-One-sip-you have to have.

MIRA. It's gross.

MISHA. Drink! You what-fourteen-You-drink! When we was fourteen, we need new liver! We pull out from throat-Squeeze like sponge-Swallow-use again.

DIANA. Okay, she drink, she drink a sip. Amaretto is for me. Everybody have? Good-Okay so … Welcome. We very happy to have you-We very happy you here —

BORIS. Spaceba — *[Thank you —]*

DIANA. And, eh — We want so you should be very successful — Eh, healthy, happy — And just remember, please — In zis country they have very special thing which is called a paternity test, okay? I'm only saying … No, I … Ya skuchala po tebye. *[I missed you.]*

BORIS. Ya toje, ochen. *[Me, too.]*

DIANA. Okay — Nazdarovya — *[Cheers.]*

ALL. Nazdarovya. *[Cheers.]*

DIANA. Hey, kak Tyotya Luba? *[Hey, how is Aunt Luba?]*

BORIS. Harosho, ti znayesh. Ee Petrovich, kak on? *[Good, you know. And Petrovich, how's he doing?]*

DIANA. Da, da, harosho— *[Yeah, yeah, good —]*

BORIS. On pryepadoyot? *[He teaches?]*

MISHA. Nyet. *[No.]* Alex, what Vladimir is doing? Petrovich? He still driving for Kings Car?

ALEX. Nah, he's uh— He's a jeweler, actually.

MISHA. Hew, hew, right. Jewelry. All of a sudden he too good for us.

ALEX. What's too good about it? Guy's a jeweller, not a fuckin' C.E.O.

MISHA. / Alex —

ALEX. Seriously, it's like he don't gotta wake up at five in the morning and drive, so now he's an asshole?

MISHA. Listen-Is-za-way-he-acting. Is question of attitude. Believe you me — Gold in za Diamond District. Gold in Chinatown. You don' see him-I-see-him. On Ocean Avenue, I see him maybe in September? Yeah, for za kolbasa he comes — For good caviar, sure. For you wedding or you funeral? Go fuck youself.

DIANA. He just bought a very nice condo —

MISHA. Mira, you friends wiz za girl-What's-her-name-za-daughter?

MIRA. Rochelle-I'm-not. They moved to Long Island, like an ice age ago, arready —

MISHA. Long Island, you see? Too good. Gotta go to Long Island, to Whitestone — To za Greeks! The kids they send upstate — Far away in za snow. *(To Mira.)* You never gonna go SUNY Buffalo, SUNY Binghamton. You gonna stay Virgin-Brooklyn-College Virgin-Hunter-College. Is long commute, but you Virgin-Hunter College.

DIANA. She's a good girl.

MIRA. No, I'm not.

DIANA. She a good / girl.

MISHA. *(To Boris.)* Okay, but serious, I'm telling you — Eta samoya lootshaya strona. *[This is the best country.]* You gonna see. This is the best country! Right, Alex? Za best!

BORIS. Yeah? You sure?

MISHA. You don' believe?

BORIS. It's country where university professor is selling jewelry.

DIANA. … Alex, maybe after dinner, you taking Boris to Sheepshead Bay? You get a coffee, maybe a drink, another one?

MIRA. Can I go, too?

DIANA. Shut up, you got school.

MIRA. So does he.

DIANA. He's an idiot. You see what's on top of his neck? It's a marshmallow. So?

ALEX. Nah, I got like a previous engagement.

DIANA. What engagement, you got?

ALEX. I'm hangin' out with Gregory.

DIANA. So Boris can go wiz you.

MISHA. Come on — He don' need some old fart around when he trying to catch za girls in / za bar —

DIANA. What you talking old — He a young guy.

MISHA. N'ye yebyey m'n'ye mozgee — *[Don't fuck with me.]*

DIANA. Don't fuck with me.

BORIS. ... This set up is good set up. Good looking bed.

DIANA. Don' worry, you upstairs. Mira down here.

MIRA. Just for tonight, I am.

DIANA. This one talks a lot-Pretend-it's a fart.

BORIS. You give up bed? This is big kindness. This is kindness, big time. When someone give up they own bed, this is like in Bible times.

MIRA. Okay, where'd you learn English so well?

BORIS. Ah. I take Oxford University course.

MIRA. Bullshit.

BORIS. I was major philosopher, I / swear.

MIRA. Whatever.

BORIS. You know Descartes? We was like zis. *(Crosses his finger.)* No, no, I was liking za books a lot when I was young.

DIANA. Yeah, but now you big shot, so you don' need them.

MISHA. Shtaw ya govoril — *[What did I say —]*

DIANA. He is. What you want from me? But you remembering you family. You remembering who change the diapers and smell you shit.

ALEX. I'm eating, here.

DIANA. Whatchu think, a baby don't take a shit when you eat? This one, his ass never stop running and I'm za one wiz za diaper. I remember. You don't forget, ah?

BORIS. I won't.

DIANA. Yeah, it's very good you here, believe me. 'Special now-Hey-tell-me, he looking a lot like you, no?

BORIS. For sure — Right here, he looking. *(He holds Alex's arm.)*

ALEX. Come on.

DIANA. You do, I'm telling you. But I mean, even more he got za same style, this one.

BORIS. Oh yeah?

DIANA. Ah-hah.

ALEX. Yeah, I got that like fresh off the boat style.

BORIS. You telling me I got zis style?

ALEX. Yo', the shoes, I mean — Come on.

MIRA. Yeah, look at your jeans.

BORIS. Shit.

DIANA. I'm not talking clothes, you know. I'm talking on za inside parts — Believe me. On za inside, wow — Is like I'm back twenty year and looking at you.

MISHA. Yeah, only you wish you not gonna have za same problems what you Mama had wiz her son, right? *(Misha laughs alone. It peters out.)*

BORIS. How, eh — How car service is doing, Misha?

DIANA. Come on, give to everyone what is like — Quarterly Report.

MISHA. Look what a bitch you sister is.

DIANA. Aei, please.

MISHA. This one, it's not enough a-house-a-car-She wanna live like a Kennedy.

DIANA. I want to live?

BORIS. Ona vsyegda billa ambeetseyozna. Doma, "ona ee shvyets, ee zh'nyets, ee na doodye eegryets." Ee yei vsyevo billo d'vyenatset l'yet." *[She was always ambitious. At home, "she sewed, she gathered wheat, and she played the trumpet." And this is before she was twelve years old.]* Wow, she don' understand. *(To Mira.)* I am saying your mother is a born businesswoman. Always. When we are little she is business. Now we are big she is business.

DIANA. Yeah, someone gotta be.

MISHA. I swear, I'm gonna —

DIANA. You gonna what? *(They eat in silence for a moment.)*

MIRA. You know, I actually might be going to Europe this summer.

MISHA. What?

DIANA. She not —

MISHA. How you going to Europe?

MIRA. It's not for sure / but —

DIANA. Listen, the only vacation she getting is the one to my asshole —

MIRA. That is so ridiculous.

DIANA. Don' worry — Now is tourist season. It's very temperate. Okay: How many decaf, how many regular?

MIRA. I'm still eating.

DIANA. So finish, whatchu on a cruise?

MISHA. You mother, she stingy like Stalin. She keeping all za bread and when you die from hungry, she cry for you.

BORIS. I have a decaf.

DIANA. Okay, one decaf. *(Misha raises his hand.)* Two, arright — Alex?

ALEX. I'm good — I'm gonna head out —

DIANA. What you talking — Come / on —

ALEX. I gotta wake up early / tomorrow —

DIANA. I bringing home apple cake from work, what / you like —

ALEX. I'll have some later —

DIANA. What / later —

MISHA. Dianachka — Leave him alone-He's-hunting-for-pussy.

MIRA. What?

MISHA. Come here. Listen: Girls-They-like-umbrella-cranberry-juice-diet-soda. You buy two three drinks wiz this. *(Misha hands Alex a twenty-dollar bill.)*

DIANA. Suddenly we got a big spender.

MISHA. You understand?

ALEX. Arright.

MISHA. Yeah?

ALEX. I got it.

MISHA. Okay so good, get out.

ALEX. Um — Hey, nice to meet you-See-you. Whatever.

BORIS. Absolute. Is very nice to be around za family, again — I'm telling you-Is-long time. Too long time. *(He hugs Alex.)*

ALEX. Oh — okay.

BORIS. You look good, yeah … Nice jacket.

ALEX. I'm tellin' you — Style, brother.

BORIS. Ah-huh.

ALEX. Arright — Peace out, bitch-es. *(Alex exits.)*

BORIS. I bring za bags up.

MISHA. Yeah, sure.

DIANA. Sadyeec, ti mozhesh zdyelat eto pozjhe — *[Sit, you can do it later —]*

BORIS. Pozvolte m'nye v'tuyalet. *[Let me use the bathroom.]* I wash up my face little bit. Is upstairs, which room?

DIANA. Mira, show him. Is very good, very comfortable. You gonna like. *(Mira gets a piece of luggage.)*

BORIS. I take, I take, don' worry.

DIANA. Ti sobirayeshcya pamoch? *[You going to help?]*

MISHA. He's getting it — Look.

MIRA. It's the first one, at the top. *(Boris and Mira go upstairs.)* How long was your flight?

BORIS. Nine and a half hour, maybe.

MIRA. Oh my God. *(Mira and Boris enter Mira's room. Mira checks the dresser.)* I think — Yeah, she cleared out the bottom two.

BORIS. Very nice. *(He puts his bag on the bed, and opens it. Mira watches him.)* What?

MIRA. Nothing. I'll see you / later —

BORIS. Wait, hold one minute, I bring something for you. *(He pulls out two packages from his luggage.)* Pick. *(She goes for one and he pulls it back. She goes for it again. The same. She takes the other one and opens it.)* You a little bigger than I was thinking, so maybe you don' need, but I don' know. Is always nice to bring something, even if is wrong, you know. *(She takes out a matryoshka doll.)* You have a lot arready, ah?

MIRA. Yeah. But I mean, thank you.

BORIS. Thank you.

MIRA. For what?

BORIS. For za room. Don' worry, I gonna be out tomorrow.

MIRA. … You swear, right?

BORIS. Absolute.

MIRA. Okay. *(She holds her pinky out.)*

BORIS. What zis?

MIRA. This is how you swear-It's-dumb-Forget it.

BORIS. No, please I need to know. I don' want I should embarrass myself.

MIRA. Um … You hold out your — Yeah. Like that. *(They pinky swear.)*

Scene 2

The next morning. In Mira's room, Boris gets dressed. Mira is sleeping on the air mattress. Alex enters and kicks the mattress. He exits to the kitchen, reenters with cereal and bowls. He kicks the mattress again.

MIRA. You're like the most inconsiderate person ever!

ALEX. Shut up.

MIRA. Stop it!

ALEX. Shut up.

MIRA. You're / such a jerk.

ALEX. Such a jerk. Get up arready.

MIRA. Don' put too much milk. I'm so tired.

ALEX. Listen, you have to take the train today.

MIRA. What — Why?

ALEX. I'm busy.

MIRA. I'm gonna tell Ma you're cutting.

ALEX. Good. Tell her.

MIRA. I'm serious.

ALEX. Me too. Call her and tell her. Right now.

MIRA. I will.

ALEX. I'm gonna dial her work. You tell her, and then I'm gonna rip your fuckin' face off.

MIRA. Alex.

ALEX. No, it's no big deal. I got a little extra time, so I can totally rip your fuckin' face off and still get to where I gotta be.

MIRA. Okay, whatever, but come on.

ALEX. I said I'm busy.

MIRA. Doing what?

ALEX. None of your business. I got a date. Like a study date. I'm doing S.A.T. training, or whatever.

MIRA. For fuckin' Kingsborough? You'll get in. I think all they do is ask for ID.

ALEX. You know what? You're ugly.

MIRA. Yeah-right-whatever.

ALEX. No. Seriously. Ugly. *(Boris enters.)*

BORIS. Eh — Coffee you having ready —

ALEX. There's instant — Uh — The water just boiled — You want / me to —

BORIS. No, I got, sit. *(Boris exits to the kitchen. Alex looks at Mira for a long moment.)*

MIRA. What?

ALEX. You really need to start wearing makeup.

MIRA. That's stupid.

ALEX. It's true. There's like scientific experiments and studies and shit, which show that people like you more if you're pretty. 'Cause you make the effort, or whatever.

MIRA. So what, I should be like Korina Lipovsky?

ALEX. Yeah, she's fuckin' hot.

MIRA. That's not her real eyes, even. She wears the colored contacts so like, the second she looks at you, you could see her fakeness.

ALEX. I'd totally do her … Look at you. Fuckin' crappy clothes — At least cover your zits. Guys don't wanna look at that, like up close.

MIRA. What guys?

ALEX. Mira.

MIRA. Alex.

ALEX. Listen, it's like with dogs, okay? You gotta take your food first. Alpha. And then you let the other dog, the loser dog eat the seconds. So, stop fuckin' eating the seconds. You're like drooling over it, it's embarrassing.

MIRA. … I have like no idea what you're talking about. *(Boris reenters.)*

ALEX. Really? You weren't behind that courtyard dumpster with Tim What-the-fuckerelli, for like two hours after school yesterday —

MIRA. Shut up —

ALEX. Just beggin' / for it —

MIRA. Alex, shut up! *(Boris sits at the table with them.)*

MIRA. … I'm gonna change. *(Mira exits.)*

BORIS. How was you night last night?

ALEX. Good, yeah.

BORIS. You don' get too, uh, too crazy, or something?

ALEX. Nah, I was home by like midnight.

BORIS. Arright, very nice … So hey, lemme ask you, you having some time for me zis week, maybe Friday?

ALEX. What for?

BORIS. Easy shit. Delivery. You busy, or what?

ALEX. I don't know — Probably.

BORIS. Probably?

ALEX. Yeah, I mean I got school.

BORIS. At night.

ALEX. I got a job —

BORIS. You working?

ALEX. Maybe. I mean if I'm not at Verizon, I'm probably gonna do some charity work next door, right?

BORIS. Okay, listen Alex. You Mama asking me for help —

ALEX. Well she asks for a lot-You-don't have to do something just 'cause she asks you. At least, I don't. Not every time, arright?

BORIS. … Arright, whatever. *(He picks up Alex's phone.)* Looks good.

ALEX. It's decent. You still got an international one, huh?

BORIS. I do.

ALEX. This one's good, but they comin' out with the new model in the spring so, definitely not worth it right now.

BORIS. Ah-huh. How much?

ALEX. The new one, with the mail-in rebate, it's gonna be one ninety-nine. But after employee discount, I can probably get it for maybe one-fifty.

BORIS. Pshh. Is always so fucking expensive, or / what —

ALEX. Actually, that's a really good deal. For what you're getting? I mean, it's sick. Plus, if you sign a two-year contract, you get a dis-counted data plan.

BORIS. I don't know. Sound like a lot to me.

ALEX. I mean, it's worth it. It's definitely worth it.

BORIS. Mm-hm. So lemme ask you question. Let say, I buy za phone, what you getting?

ALEX. What do you mean?

BORIS. Like you getting a cut from this or what?

ALEX. I get a commission, sure —

BORIS. / Ah-huh —

ALEX. I mean, not since I'm using my discount, but normally / sure —

BORIS. Yeah — So what like ten percent?

ALEX. Ten percent?

BORIS. More?

ALEX. They'd never turn a profit, if they gave you / ten —

BORIS. So, less?

ALEX. Yeah. Five percent per unit.

BORIS. Sure, sure. Crazy country. For finding me a phone, you get money to help wiz bills, wiz food shopping, and also to pay for such nice Diesel jacket what you wear last night? I don' think so.

ALEX. ... I guess I'm just really good at my job.

BORIS. Yeah, of course, okay — But for here, this place — Za mortgage is two thousand five hundred. Car service bringing in nothing — In fact is costing, right? So, this a lot of expenses what you having. A lot of overhead. For money like this, I'm thinking, you gotta sell more than a phone. I'm thinking you gotta sell cocaine ... Or just marijuana you sell?

ALEX. ... I'm not —

BORIS. Don't.

ALEX. It's not —

BORIS. Alex. Don't.

ALEX. ... Are you gonna tell Ma?

BORIS. I don' know.

ALEX. Are you gonna tell her, or what?

BORIS. She my sister. I have reason not to tell something?

ALEX. This is fuckin' ... Fuck!

BORIS. Listen —

ALEX. She won't care, I'm doin'-it-Seriously-I mean Pop, maybe, but not her.

BORIS. Okay, so then what is problem?

ALEX. What is ... She arready gets everything I make from the store — Last month she asked me for my pay stub, to check, to make sure. I mean, what I make from that other stuff —

BORIS. From selling drugs —

ALEX. Yeah, whatever, it's mine, okay?

BORIS. What zis bullshit mine? Everybody working off they ass 'round here, but for you is more important fancy clothes? / Come on —

ALEX. Okay, first of all, I'm one of those people. I got two fuckin' jobs, school, and you're sayin' I don't give a shit? And it's not just clothes, arright? I got a buddy from the store, older guy — Just bought a house in Dyker Heights, he's renovating the upstairs apartment, but like when it's done, fuckin' forget it.

BORIS. So this what you saving for?

ALEX. Basically, he guaranteed it to me — Like he ain't even gonna list it. I just gotta come up with first month plus security deposit.

BORIS. Fine, so look. What I'm telling you — You can be making more, if you want to be helping me.

ALEX. Bullshit.

BORIS. Not bullshit.

ALEX. If I work for you, she gets every fucking penny that hits my hand and you know it. Lemme ask you, you arready tell her how much you gonna pay me? Yeah, thought so. *(Mira reenters.)*

MIRA. Can you at least drop me by the train station?

ALEX. Shut up!

MIRA. I didn't do anything!

ALEX. You fuckin' started existing! *(Alex exits to the kitchen.)*

MIRA. … You are like so lucky, you get to stay home … You should make Tater Tots.

BORIS. I will. Thank you.

MIRA. … Hey, you've been all over the world, right?

BORIS. I go only to beautiful places.

MIRA. Can I ask you something?

BORIS. I don't know if I can answer.

MIRA. Is blue my color?

BORIS. Blue?

MIRA. Yeah. Is this my color? *(She holds her arms out.)*

BORIS. Of course.

MIRA. Really?

BORIS. No question.

MIRA. I thought it was, but…

BORIS. What?

MIRA. Nothing… But you think this is good on me, right?

BORIS. This is tops.

MIRA. Okay. *(Alex reenters.)*

ALEX. Get your shit. I gotta get to the store.

MIRA. Verizon doesn't even open until like ten o'clock. Who buys a cell phone at seven-thirty in the morning?

ALEX. I'm serious!

BORIS. Mira, he is businessman, you brother. He got a lot of activities, right, Sasha?

ALEX. No one calls me that.

BORIS. No?

ALEX. Not since we left Russia, okay?

BORIS. My apologize.

ALEX. You're gonna be late.

MIRA. So?

ALEX. So, I'm the one who's gonna get shit for it. Let's go. Come on!

MIRA. Fine! *(She exits.)*

ALEX. It's like now I got three of you, I gotta …

BORIS. Listen, I'm a lucky guy, arright. Very lucky. I want to move here, I can. Lot of guys I know, they can' be doing this. Only reason why I can — Only reason is I have family, right? So, she ask me for a favor, you mama — What I can say to her?

ALEX. That's great. So you have to do her a favor, and I'm the one who gets dicked over — Awesome. Story of my fuckin' life.

BORIS. No one getting dicked over —

ALEX. Sounds like I'm getting another job, right? Tell me again how no one's getting —

BORIS. Okay, how much you make on a good week?

ALEX. Doing what?

BORIS. Selling.

ALEX. Oh. Depends on how much I can get, depends if it's good. I don't know, one-fifty?

BORIS. That's it?

ALEX. Man, it's just dime bags. Whatever my manager has left over from the weekend.

BORIS. Okay. So I told Mama, you will be making two hundred per job. Thing is, she don' know how many jobs you going to do. Like, let say I have three next week, but she only know about one. Good deal for you, right?

ALEX. … Why would you do that?

BORIS. I have no fucking idea. *(He smiles. They share a moment.)* Maybe I do, I don' know yet.

ALEX. You won't tell her about —

BORIS. I don' tell her shit.

ALEX. … Okay.

BORIS. But you don' take advantage, right? Little bit extra, just for you.

ALEX. Commission.

BORIS. Right. So, you got some time this weekend, or what?

ALEX. I mean, I guess.

BORIS. You guess or you know?

ALEX. No I do, I — Yes, I do — Okay.

BORIS. Great, I get wiz my guy today and I let you know. Probably Friday, I have like airport pickup for you —

ALEX. Whoa, hold up. An airport pickup?

BORIS. Ah-hah —

ALEX. I don't — I mean …

BORIS. What?

ALEX. That's like serious shit.

BORIS. Nah, nah, nah —

ALEX. The fuckin' airport?

BORIS. Look, you don' even get out za car. Is same thing what you doing for you little business. Pick up and move. Only now is what-you-call: Freelance Contract … I tell you where you need to be, which terminal. Hey. You my sister-son, right?

ALEX. Uh-huh.

BORIS. So, come on. You take what they give you and bring to za address what I tell you.

ALEX. And then just do a drop off.

BORIS. Yeah.

ALEX. … Arright.

BORIS. Perfect. You can give me a ride, or —

ALEX. Uh, yeah. I just gotta pick up my — My stuff for the week. But he'll wait a few. Where you going?

BORIS. I have here za — Coney Island Avenue and Avenue Z — Alina's — You know where is?

ALEX. Yeah, that's — That's a bar.

BORIS. Ah-huh, right.

ALEX. You goin' to a bar at eight in the morning?

BORIS. You can drop me off. I get a ride back, don' worry. *(Boris gets his coat and puts on his shoes. No socks.)* You know, I am used to snow on bare feet. This is reminding me of home a little. Same kind of burning. You remember home?

ALEX. A little. Not really.

BORIS. Of course. You are too young. Listen, my first side business, also I start I was maybe little older than you, maybe twenty. Is smart thing, trust me.

ALEX. Well, you heard my mother. I'm a fuckin' genius.

BORIS. … Arright, where you car?

ALEX. It's out front.

BORIS. Key. Yes. Okay. *(Boris exits.)* Alex!

ALEX. I'm comin'. *(Alex exits. Transition: The office. The phone rings. Misha enters and hustles for it. He picks it up.)*

MISHA. 'Allo? … 'Allo? *(He hangs up and looks through some drawers. The phone rings.)* 'Allo? … 'Allo — Eta ktaw? … Eta ktaw? [Who's this? … Who is this?] (He hangs up. He continues searching through drawers and finds a set of keys. The phone rings. He looks at it for a while. He picks up the receiver and hangs up. He exits.)*

Scene 3

Mira's bedroom. Mira knocks on the door then enters. She gets a few books from the desk. She sees Boris' phone. She flips it open. Boris appears in the doorway in boxer shorts, a white T-shirt, carrying a towel. He gets dressed during the scene.

BORIS. Hi —

MIRA. Oh, hey — I didn't know you were home. Sorry, I was getting some / things.

BORIS. Is okay —

MIRA. Sorry.

BORIS. You coming to kick me out?

MIRA. I guess.

BORIS. Listen, I still having to go DMV, today. Maybe you can wait few hour? I get home, pack up.

MIRA. Like how long you think you'll be?

BORIS. Like few hour.

MIRA. Oh, yeah — Right. No problem.

BORIS. Okay, thanks. You need to make phone call?

MIRA. What? No I was um — I was just, uh — Because of the whole … *(He lets her off the hook.)* Okay … So who is that?

BORIS. What?

MIRA. Your wallpaper.

BORIS. Friend of mine.

MIRA. Like your girlfriend? *(He shakes his head.)* What? Is she like a hook-up, or something?

BORIS. What zis?

MIRA. Oh, it's like if you don't want a long term commitment or whatever and you're just, you know … like messing around and … I dunno …

BORIS. You do this wiz boys?

MIRA. No.

BORIS. Okay.

MIRA. What?

BORIS. Nothing.

MIRA. Okay-wait-hold-on, Alex? He just says shit, like all the time. And just 'cause he says it doesn't mean it's true. I mean reality is so much more, like complicated, and there are just layers of meaning that you can't … I'm sorry, I really don't want to talk about it.

BORIS. Hey listen, boys don't know special. When they young is only bam, bam, bam. No thinking, only going. They gonna know soon.

MIRA. Whatever … So who is she?

BORIS. Just a girl.

MIRA. That you keep a picture of. That's kind of romantic. When was the last time you saw her?

BORIS. I don't know-Long-time-Hey-I-want to ask you — Where you going in Europe?

MIRA. Oh. Florence. I mean if they accept me.

BORIS. Is a beautiful city.

MIRA. Have you been?

BORIS. Sure, I was few time, arready. It was tops. When you going?

MIRA. Well, it's like a summer semester thing? Like this one is for art history, and you stay in Florence but then you go all over. And you can get credit for when you go to college.

BORIS. Very smart thing.

MIRA. Right?

BORIS. Absolute. You on za ball.

MIRA. You should totally tell my mother that.

BORIS. I don't know I can tell her anything. She a scary woman.

MIRA. Omigod, she's such a fascist. But she would listen to you, I mean, I really think she would … Forget it, you're bullshitting me.

BORIS. No, no, no — Travel is important for young girl. You are having to see, before you are married, pyramids, Alps mountains —

MIRA. Before you're married?

BORIS. Yeah. What?

MIRA. Nothing. *(They look at each other for a moment.)* I should go, I got homework. *(She lingers.)* We're reading Mark Twain-you-ever-read-Mark-Twain?

BORIS. No.

MIRA. Omigod, don't. It's so weird. All they do is like go to church and paint fences and stuff.

BORIS. In school we read Pushkin, Dostoyevsky.

MIRA. Yeah, I also have to. But not 'til sophomore year. But the cover is like wei-erd. *Crime and Punishment.*

BORIS. *Prestuplenye i Nakazaniye. [Crime and Punishment.]*

MIRA. Yeah. It's a redhead, with an ax like half-way in his head, and I'm like, "Hello, I'm a minor." You should see it. It's stupid creepy. *(She pulls open a drawer in the desk. She closes the drawer. He comes up behind her.)* ... I'll go, I got ... work, I —

BORIS. For art history, you got?

MIRA. *(Turning to face him.)* What — Yeah ... Excuse me —

BORIS. In Russia, I am like you, like artistichisky *[Artistic.]* But here ... everyone is driver, some shit. Shostakovich come to New York? I guarantee he is medical assistant, no?

MIRA. Totally.

BORIS. So I don't know. Maybe I'm also gonna be driver, whatchu think?

MIRA. Sure.

BORIS. I am asking for opinion.

MIRA. Oh ... Um, you could get a job with the MTA? My dad's cousin Greesha did, and, uh ... It's good to work for the city — they give benefits.

BORIS. Ah, very nice. There is a line for this job? Or phone number? Maybe Greesha talk to them for me.

MIRA. Sure. *(He opens the drawer and takes out a gun.)* There's-also-a-test-you-gotta-take. *(He makes a move to put the gun in her hand. She resists.)*

BORIS. Okay. *(He makes a show of releasing the ammunition.)*

MIRA. I really have a lot of work. I'm in two A.P. classes. *(He puts the unloaded gun in her hand.)*

BORIS. Mama tell you I was in jail? ... Is embarrassment. For her, for me even more. I steal parts of car, stupid, stupid. You ever do something you are ashamed from?

MIRA. I don't know ... I guess.

BORIS. Yeah, everyone do. Don' worry, mistakes is making you smart. *(He cups the hand with which she holds the gun.)* See? Nothing. *(He lifts it up and down easily. He smiles.)* Mirachka. Spakoina. *[Relax.]* You know what's spakoina? *(She nods.)* What, tell me?

MIRA. Relax.

BORIS. About everything, I mean. Serious. You nervous like you Mama. *(He reloads the gun and puts it away.)* I am curious what you do, it makes you ashame? *(She shrugs.)* Wiz boyfriend?

MIRA. No-o.

BORIS. Okay, okay, I see. Listen. I tell you because we friends, okay? Boys, they are stupid. Something is happening when you are adult, like you learn how to be with girls. You learn you gotta listen. You learn you don't make them cry. Only sometimes is strange … Nothing.

MIRA. No, what?

BORIS. Sometimes … You want to make them cry. The face is red then. It's bright, so they are more beautiful. So sometimes you make them cry, but this is not for fun. You only want to see something beautiful. *(She looks at him. They are very close. She kisses him. It goes on for a second, then he turns his face away.)*

MIRA. I'm sorry.

BORIS. Is okay.

MIRA. I'm really sorry —

BORIS. Don' worry 'bout it. I move my things when I come home, arright?

MIRA. Yeah, don't … I mean, whenever is fine — You can stay a little while if you … Okay. *(She goes to the door.)*

BORIS. Mira. You won't tell anyone, right?

MIRA. What? *(He touches the drawer.)* Oh. No.

BORIS. Good. *(Mira exits as lights transition to car. She is now Sonya.)*

Scene 4

SONYA. Buick LeSabre, 363?

ALEX. Yeah, thas' me.

SONYA. Ah, you are Victor?

ALEX. Oh, no I'm just — I'm just takin' / you —

SONYA. Okay, yes — Menya zavoot Sonya. *[I'm Sonya.]*

ALEX. Hey. Alex.

SONYA. Hello.

ALEX. Hey. So, um, you got any luggage or anything?

SONYA. Eh, what is?

ALEX. Bagazja, yest? *[Luggage, you have?]*

SONYA. I giving to za man.

ALEX. Oh, cool / arright —

SONYA. He bringing in he car.

ALEX. Awesome. So you're good — I mean, you went to the bathroom and everything? Too-alet? *[Bathroom?]*

SONYA. Mnye ne nado. *[I don't have to.]*

ALEX. You sure? It's just they told me not to stop and the drive's like an hour if there's no traffic. I mean, there shouldn't be but if there's an accident and if you got something like up your — I mean, inside you, or whatever — I don't know, maybe it's uncomfortable, I guess …

SONYA. We going, or no?

ALEX. Yes. Forget it — Yes. *(He drives.)*

ALEX. Ty v poryadke, yesli ya v'kluchayu radio? *[You okay if I turn on the radio?]*

SONYA. Da, pazhalasta. *[Yeah, please.]* *(He turns on the radio.)*

ALEX. You had a good trip over? Haroshi-y palyot? *[Good flight?]*

SONYA. *(Nods.)* Ah.

ALEX. It's long as shit, right?

SONYA. Mm-hm. Mnye holodno. *[I'm cold.]*

ALEX. Oh, sorry. *(He turns up the heat.)* Yeah, I usually keep it pretty cold. It's like refreshing-and-what-not —

SONYA. We seeing Fifth Avenue?

ALEX. What?

SONYA. Fifth Avenue?

ALEX. Like, in the City?

SONYA. Mm, Rockefeller, Saks, we see?

ALEX. No, it's not —

SONYA. Please?

ALEX. Um, we're actually going to New Jersey.

SONYA. New Jersey?

ALEX. Yeah.

SONYA. Why?

ALEX. I know, right? It's — Nothing, stupid. We're not driving through Manhattan.

SONYA. Shtaw? *[What?]*

ALEX. Eto na putye. *[It's not on the way.]*

SONYA. Oh. I wanting to see mm — Lot. Everything, I wanting. Fast, fast, fast. Now to see.

ALEX. Sure, yeah. So is this — Is this your first time in New York? Ti perviey ras zdyes? *[Your first time here?]*

SONYA. Da, kanyeshna. *[Yes, absolutely.]*

ALEX. Cool, arright — Well, I'm gonna go through Staten Island, so I think you could see the Statue of Liberty.

SONYA. Ah, yes? Okay, wow.

ALEX. I'll let you know when we're passing it. It actually looks really small from there. I don't know how, like, Impressive it'll be. … You know it's funny, when you go inside, like they used to let you go to the top before 9/11 —

SONYA. 9/11 yes, I know.

ALEX. Yeah. So, I mean I went with school when I was a kid. And it takes forever. The line moves crazy slow, but the whole time you're like, "Oh man, I'm gonna get to look out The Statue of Liberty," but you get to the top and it's just like a dirty window … Anyway, don't be disappointed if you see it and you're not like, taken aback or whatever. Probably happens a lot.

SONYA. Mm, I sorry, I no understanding.

ALEX. Ya skazjoo tyebye kogda. *[I'll let you know when.]*

SONYA. Statue of Liberty?

ALEX. Yeah. I'll let you know.

SONYA. Okay. Oh, I can ask you — Kogda ya paloochyoo moiy passpart? *[When do I get my passport back?]*

ALEX. Huh?

SONYA. I would like, please.

ALEX. Um, I don't like, have your passport.

SONYA. Oh. Victor has?

ALEX. I guess. Maybe. Like, maybe you give him the stuff and he gives you your passport, or something? I don't know … I'm not normally like International? Like you know when people say "Buy local"? Tha's me, I'm for local businesses. It's really big, now.

SONYA. Eh, I no understand —

ALEX. Man, you really gotta learn some English. Zucheet Engliski *[Learn English.]*

SONYA. I learning.

ALEX. Good, it's like the universal language. They speak it everywhere. Speak it in like India, France. Everywhere.

SONYA. Is important for business.

ALEX. Oh for you, no doubt. I mean, you probably travel a lot, like with the / whole —

SONYA. And also, I learning Italian, little bit.

ALEX. Okay, I guess that would be helpful in like, Italy.

SONYA. You want hearing what I knowing?

ALEX. Sure, lay it out.

SONYA. Queste sono le mie foto.

ALEX. Shit. What's that mean?

SONYA. This is my pictures.

ALEX. This is my pictures? Man you gotta know how to say like, "Where's the bathroom?" or like I don't know — Somethin' it's actually gonna help you out. Zucheet vasnye voche. *[Learn important things.]*

SONYA. This important for model.

ALEX. *(Laughing.)* Oh yeah, whatayou a model?

SONYA. Of course.

ALEX. … Okay.

SONYA. … I like, I like. You can make — *(She motions for him to turn up the radio.)*

ALEX. Uh, yeah.

SONYA. She my best. Selena Gomez? I love. Love, love, love.

ALEX. Yeah, she's um — So are you gonna do that here?

SONYA. Doing?

ALEX. Modeling, or whatever.

SONYA. I hoping, yes. Very much, I hoping.

ALEX. Uh-huh —

SONYA. They tell me is will be lot of work for me, now / so.

ALEX. Who told you —

SONYA. Man from model agency. Who sending me here. He discovering all big-time Russian models. And before? He working wiz Heidi Klum.

ALEX. … Fuck.

SONYA. … Wow. This is East River, yes?

ALEX. No, it's … Jamaica Bay.

SONYA. Okay, I see. *(Driving.)*

ALEX. Sonya? Um … So, how old are you?

SONYA. Mmm.

ALEX. Tyebye skolka lyet? *[How old are you?]*

SONYA. Numbers is hard / for me —
ALEX. Just tell me in Russian —
SONYA. Pyetnatsit. *[Sixteen.]*
ALEX. Oh, fuck.
SONYA. ... Hey, you telling me we seeing something, okay? Something special.
ALEX. I will. It's a pretty boring drive, but ... I will, sure.
SONYA. Thank you.
ALEX. ... You warm enough?
SONYA. Mm-hm.
ALEX. Good. *(Lights fade.)*

Scene 5

Diana pays bills at the dining room table while Mira does her homework.

DIANA. Lemme ask you, you ever wake up in za middle of night and turn on za heat?
MIRA. No.
DIANA. You know, is shutting off at ten o'clock 'cause everyone go to bed.
MIRA. Yeah.
DIANA. And if you cold, you go to za hall closet and I got good blankets. Very heavy. You don' need to come down here and futz wiz thermometer / okay?
MIRA. I didn't futz with / anything.
DIANA. No? Well someone is doing, I don' know who. Hey what you gonna wear for Sonya bat mitzvah?
MIRA. Eww, why I even gotta go to that?
DIANA. She you cousin. You not gonna go?
MIRA. I haven't seen her in like three years.
DIANA. Hey, I have to go-you-have-to-go.
MIRA. Yeah, but ... She's kind of a bitch.
DIANA. She take after her mother. That whole side za family, you know. Is just nasty people.

MIRA. Uh-huh.

DIANA. Tyotya Gala? I'm telling you, every time I'm running into her in fruit store is like tornado in my face. She talking 'bout her daughter — Non. Stop. *(Boris comes down the stairs.)* Hey, Tyotya Gala.

BORIS. Bozhemoiy. *[My God.]* Don' start.

DIANA. See, he tell you, too.

BORIS. Shit, is like next time I see her she will having to tell me everything from last twenty years what I miss.

DIANA. Kanyeshna. *[For sure.]* Eh, ti pozdna rabotayesh? *[Hey, you working late or what?]*

BORIS. N'ye znayoo. *[I don't know.]*

DIANA. Lemme give you something to take wiz you.

BORIS. Ti nye doljna — *[You don' have to —]*

DIANA. I pack it up, in case you want later —

BORIS. Da pravda, nye nuzhna — *[Seriously, I don't need —]*

DIANA. Spaokoisa! *[Relax!]* *(She exits to the kitchen. Boris sits next to Mira, putting his shoes on.)*

BORIS. How you doing?

MIRA. Good.

BORIS. Good.

MIRA. … So, where you workin'?

BORIS. Ah, just — Part time I finding.

MIRA. Oh yeah?

BORIS. Yeah, friend from home, he got a bar.

MIRA. Are you like, bartending or something?

BORIS. Little bit. Also, by za door I standing.

MIRA. … Sure, whatever.

BORIS. Why? You wanna come in?

MIRA. To a bar?

BORIS. Yeah.

MIRA. Okay.

BORIS. Great, any time. You let me know.

MIRA. I don't have an ID.

BORIS. Yeah, but you know guy by za door. Is all you ever need. You want come in, you just send me za text, I wait outside for you.

MIRA. Whatever.

BORIS. Serious.

MIRA. Okay. Okay, so give me your number.

BORIS. Yeah, no problem. You give me yours, also. *(They take out their phones.)*

MIRA. When'd you get that?

BORIS. Nice, right —

MIRA. Yeah.

BORIS. You brother get for me. Is got za video, za GPS —

MIRA. I know, I been trying to convince him to get me one.

BORIS. And he won't? Little shit — Arright, I talk to him for you. Here. *(They switch phones and put each other's numbers in. They trade back.)* Hold on. I take picture, so I see you when you calling. Come on. Smile. *(Diana stands in the doorway, as Boris takes the picture.)* Nice.

DIANA. … Sa-lad Olivye.

BORIS. Oh my God, arright. Bolshoyo spaceba, daragaya. Ooveedyemcya zaftra. *[Thanks a lot, darling. See you, tomorrow.]* *(He exits. Diana sits back down. They work. Mira gets a text. She checks it, laughs. Diana looks at her. Back to work. Alex enters the office, comes into the house.)*

DIANA. Hey, you.

ALEX. Hi.

DIANA. You got a good night. Was bad wiz za weather or, what?

ALEX. Huh?

DIANA. On you way home.

ALEX. Oh. It was fine. Is Boris upstairs?

DIANA. No, he going out.

MIRA. He went to work.

ALEX. … Right. Did he say when he was gonna be back?

MIRA. Probably late. He's bartending.

ALEX. He's what?

DIANA. Get me some stamps.

MIRA. I'm not a butler.

DIANA. Get me some stamps before I pull you fingernails out. *(Mira exits to the kitchen.)* Front pocket of my bag!

ALEX. Where'd he really go?

DIANA. I look like za gatekeeper? Who knows. Do me a favor, put what you making away up top. From tonight, he told me you got something. *(Alex looks at her awhile, then puts the money in the envelope. Misha enters the office in darkness.)* You got indigestion, or something? Come here … You wanna Pepto?

MISHA. Alex!

DIANA. Oh my God, he probably have some needlepoint he want you should be doing. Have some seltzer, you gonna be tip

38

top. *(Mira enters with stamps.)*

MIRA. You got right here.

DIANA. They is a lot of paperwork, what I'm wading through. I probably gonna need more.

MISHA. Alex!

DIANA. Okay, go see what he want, go, go, go. *(To Mira.)* How is coming with you work?

MIRA. I got French still, and geometry —

DIANA. I don' need specifics. Good or finished is fine.

MIRA. Good. *(Alex goes enters the office. Misha drinks, facing upstage. It's dim.)*

ALEX. What's up?

MISHA. You make up za schedule for next week?

ALEX. I'll do it tomorrow.

MISHA. Is having to be posted tomorrow, else I'm gonna hear za crying from everyone! *(Alex sits at the desk.)* Where you coming from? Zev tell me he don' see you all night.

ALEX. Nowhere, I was … with Gregory.

MISHA. Yeah?

ALEX. We were at his place watchin' the game.

MISHA. No shit, he got MSG network?

ALEX. Uh-huh.

MISHA. Rangers, Anaheim, no?

ALEX. Yeah.

MISHA. Who won?

ALEX. … We didn't finish watching.

MISHA. Get out.

ALEX. Nah, his mom came home, and I …

MISHA. You know, I always like zis kid, Gregory. Always I like someone who he got za lazy eye — I don' know why. Hey, get yourself a glass.

ALEX. I'm / arright —

MISHA. Come on —

ALEX. Pop, I really / don't —

MISHA. Unless you a gay, or something. If you a gay, I understand you don' want vodka. Maybe you want a Virginia Slim instead.

ALEX. Look, I'm just gonna finish this before school —

MISHA. / Wait —

ALEX. I'll get it up by seven, I promise —

MISHA. Alex wait. Let say some of za guys — They start waving they hands at you zis week — Making some noise — You tell them is will only be a few day more.

ALEX. / What?

MISHA. You say is problem wiz za bank, but they gonna get by end of za week —

ALEX. Whatyou talking / about?

MISHA. For payroll. I moving a few things around, I having to.

ALEX. Pop.

MISHA. Okay, listen — *(He turns. He's been punched.)*

ALEX. Holy shit. *(Alex turns on the overhead light.)* What happened to your face?

MISHA. Nothing, is nothing —

ALEX. Did you get mugged / or —

MISHA. Yeah, I get mugged!

ALEX. / Jesus —

MISHA. I'm telling you on za streets is gangs — Like Somalia — Is police state on Sheepshead Bay Road! I'm in Dunkin' Donuts and they come at you-knives-guns!

ALEX. What the fuck are you talking / about?

DIANA. 'Allo?

MISHA. Big knife! Machete! *(Diana and Mira enter.)*

DIANA. Bo zjemoiy. *[My God.]*

MIRA. Oh my God.

DIANA. Shtaw sloocheelace? *[What happened?]*

MISHA. Nu, shtaw sloocheelace? *[Nu, what happened?]*

MIRA. Ma —

DIANA. Go inside, go inside —

MIRA. Get off me — Stop!

DIANA. Let's go / come on — *(She pushes Mira out of the office.)*

ALEX. Pop, just si' / down —

DIANA. You got za concussion / something —

MISHA. From only a punch? I'm a bull, I'm telling you! I run in Pamplona — You know where is Spain?

DIANA. Pachemoo ti n(y)e mog poprosit oo Borisa? *[Why couldn't you just ask Boris?]*

MISHA. Because I got standards.

DIANA. Awn moi brat — Ti dumayesh on bi n'ye — *[He's my brother — You think he wouldn't —]*

MISHA. I'm not taking shit from you brother!

ALEX. Pop, what the fuck?

40

DIANA. So, tell him, he you business partner —

MISHA. Listen, in za morning I tell za guys they having paycheck on Monday. On Monday, we say Wednesday —

DIANA. Oh, they gonna / love that —

MISHA. Wednesday, we say tomorrow, ti panyemayesh? *[You understand?]*

ALEX. I don't get it —

MISHA. By Thursday, I gonna be good —

ALEX. Why do you have to do that?

MISHA. Don' ask —

ALEX. Why?

DIANA. Because he borrowing, Alex! ... He got his hand out so far, he don' even know how many fingers he having.

ALEX. ... Pop —

DIANA. Go see you sister, arright.

ALEX. But —

DIANA. Go. *(Alex exits to the living room, and catches Mira running upstairs. He follows her to her room.)*

ALEX. Mira!

MISHA. Thank you very much, Medusa —

DIANA. You a major piece of shit you / know.

MISHA. Well, you za biggest bitch I ever met.

ALEX. Mira.

MISHA. Leave it. *(Diana tends to Misha's head. He is reluctant, but she is tender with him. He surrenders. Alex and Mira sit on her bed. He takes her hand. Lights fade.)*

End of Act One

ACT TWO

Scene 1

In the car. Alex and the second girl.

ALEX. Otkuda te? *[Where you from?]*
VERA. Kirova. *[Kirov.]*
ALEX. No way. Ya iz Smolenska. *[I'm from Smolensk.]*
VERA. Ah, pravda? *[Oh really?]*
ALEX. Da, pravda. No ya bil zdyes v'syu moyu zhizn. *[Yeah, totally. But I been here my whole life.]*
VERA. Wow. You a real New Yorker.
ALEX. Yeah.
VERA. Ti nikogda ne vernoolsya? *[You never went back?]*
ALEX. Nyet. *[No.]* No, I don' even really remember it. *(Driving.)*
VERA. Prastee. *[Excuse me.]*
ALEX. Da? *[Yes?]*
VERA. Mogoo lye ya ispolzovat tvoi mobilniy? *[May I use your mobile?]*
ALEX. Um —
VERA. Telephone? You understand telephone?
ALEX. Yeah, no I uh … Nye mogu. *[I can't.]*
VERA. Ah, no? Moya Mama valnooyetsa. *[My mother worries.]* Eh … She like me call to her I go someplace. Always. Even little place I go, she like me call to her.
ALEX. Yeah? She pushy, or what? Uh — *(She doesn't understand and he mimes a yelling mother.)*
VERA. Oh. Yes.
ALEX. Mine, too.
VERA. You mother?
ALEX. Uh-huh, totally.
VERA. So I would like talk to her. Please.
ALEX. Yeah, no I just … Razredeelac batareika. *[It's out of battery.]* I'm an idiot — I forgot to charge it.

42

VERA. Oh …

ALEX. But like, we're almost there. Pyat minoot. *[Five minutes.]*

VERA. Um …

ALEX. Ti v'poryadke? *[You okay?]*

VERA. No, I not okay — I want please you should stop.

ALEX. V'chem dyelo? *[What's wrong?]*

VERA. Me mozhem ostanovit'sya? *[Can we stop?]*

ALEX. Are you nervous, or something? Nyervnyichayesh? *[Nervous?]*

VERA. Eh … little bit, I am. Yes.

ALEX. Well, listen — You don' need to be nervous around me, right?

VERA. I … I never going before. No airplane. Only train and car. Man by za airport, who he talk wiz me … He not so nice.

ALEX. That guy? He always talks like that. On svolach. *[He's an asshole.]* Asshole. Ve mozjesh skazat? *[Can you say that?]*

VERA. Shtaw? *[What?]*

ALEX. Ve mozhen skazat "asshole"? *[Can you say "asshole"?]*

VERA. Kanyeshna. *[Of course.]* Asshole.

ALEX. That's good. You gotta learn all the important words first.

VERA. Kakie slova? *[Which words?]*

ALEX. Glavniye. *[The important ones.]* Like, uh — Okay — Dick.

VERA. Dick. Eta shtaw? *[This is what?]*

ALEX. Huye.

VERA. Ah, okay. Dick.

ALEX. Mudak. Bastard.

VERA. Bastard.

ALEX. Yeah, that's like old fashioned.

VERA. Kak skazat Yob t'vayomat? *[How do you say motherfucker?]*

ALEX. Whoa, look at you.

VERA. Sorry.

ALEX. Nah, nah, it's uh — It's motherfucker.

VERA. Motherfucker.

ALEX. Uh-uh. But fuck is pretty good 'cause you can use it a lot of different ways. Like, oslayob. Donkey fucker. Sye'eebis. Get the fuck out. So, you know, in English it really — It covers a lot.

VERA. So, fuck.

ALEX. Nice.

VERA. Kak tyebya zavut? *[What's your name?]*

ALEX. … Sasha.

VERA. Ya Vera. *[I'm Vera.]*

ALEX. Nice to meet you. Can you say that?

VERA. Nice to meet you. So tell me, I will be needing to know this for work?

ALEX. Huh?

VERA. Fuck, dick, bastard —

ALEX. Oh yeah, totally. I mean like with photographers. Those guys'll try shit. Is this — Wait a minute, is this your first time?

VERA. First time, what?

ALEX. Ti nikogda nye bila modelyoo? *[You never modeled?]*

VERA. Nyet. *[No.]*

ALEX. *You've* never modeled?

VERA. No.

ALEX. Wow, I — totally thought you'd done this before.

VERA. Why?

ALEX. 'Cause you're beautiful — I mean, you're …

VERA. Ti v'poryadke? *[You okay?]*

ALEX. Yeah, v polnom poryadke. *[Totally]* I was just thinkin'.

VERA. O Chom ti dumayesh? *[What are you thinking?]*

ALEX. Nichivaw. *[Nothing.]* I was wondering if I should … Take the Grand Central.

VERA. Sasha? I not so nervous like I am just now.

ALEX. Good, yeah that's good.

VERA. Mm-hm. Thank you.

ALEX. Oh, don' worry 'bout it.

VERA. No, you — You nice guy.

ALEX. Thanks.

VERA. Yeah. You not dick. *(Alex looks ahead as lights fade.)*

Scene 2

Diana enters with groceries. Boris is upstairs getting ready to go out. He is wearing a suit.

DIANA. 'Allo?! Mira!

BORIS. Nyet yeyo! *[She's not home!]*

DIANA. Ti ostayoshcya na obed? *[You staying for dinner?]*

BORIS. Nyet! Ya ooje na vihode! *[No! I'm on my way out!]* (He comes down the stairs.)

DIANA. Hello, James Bond. What zis, you have going on?

BORIS. Nothing, shtaw? *[What?]*

DIANA. Lemme see. You going to a wedding, or something?

BORIS. Come on.

DIANA. Look at you, Susie Q. Shtaw eta? *[What's this?]*

BORIS. Ti pomniyesh Vasyu Batkina? *[You remember Vasya Batkin?]*

DIANA. Vasya Batkin — Ukranskiye Vasya? *[Ukrainian Vasya?]*

BORIS. Yeah, yeah. He having his birthday by za Buchari tonight.

DIANA. No shit. I was thinking he living in New Jersey.

BORIS. He was, but now he by Kings Highway.

DIANA. Oh, is like he move in za opposite direction.

BORIS. What you getting, anything good?

DIANA. Yeah, by za bakery they opening up like superstore. Take, you want something. They making okay za vinyigret, but you having to be very careful what you buy, because sometime they telling you is chicken salad, but really is all tomato — Maybe three piece chicken.

BORIS. I don' know, is tasting different everything here ... Hey you know who is Anton Malkov?

DIANA. ... Yeah.

BORIS. Yeah.

DIANA. How you know him?

BORIS. I don't. I never talk to him before. I just know he living at 4925 Coyle Street. And he having three kids and a wife. And he driving a Toyota Corolla, which if you asking me, is not za best way to like present youself to za world.

DIANA. Okay, no thank you.

BORIS. I can talk to him.

DIANA. No.

BORIS. You know how much he still owe, you husband?

DIANA. Take a napkin.

BORIS. Listen, I go over his house one time, this Anton — Tomorrow even I can go —

DIANA. You dripping on my table —

BORIS. One time. Slushei — *[Listen —]* Guy like him? He shit his pants before you ring za bell. You husband don' have to find out it was me.

DIANA. Yeah, of course — Is gonna be like magic. Listen, you doing for Alex, is enough. Better you don' touch car service, or I never gonna to hear za end of it. Joan of Arc, next door — He very picky about who he stick his hand out to.

BORIS. So why you have to suffer because he picky?

DIANA. I don' suffer because of my husband, I suffer because I'm breathing. Is like a coat I got, you know? Outside is always gonna be snowing shit, so I making sure I wear something warm.

BORIS. Bo zhemoy. *[My God.]* Both of you. You know how much I was making ten years ago? Five hundred thousand. Okay so here is nothing — How much this is in dollars?

DIANA. Do I look like Citibank?

BORIS. Okay fine, but at home — I mean, I can pay for whole other flat — Nice, one bedroom. And like for years I was telling Mama — You can leave — I help you, right? You don' have to wait around until you husband gonna die — Take his shit for another twenty years. But she — You know, she can' do it, and then is too late.

DIANA. Okay, I tell you what. You get me an apartment — Three bedroom — On za beach, elevator building, parking —

BORIS. / Shut up —

DIANA. I leave my husband, my kids — I get two dogs. Everybody have they own room. Hey. *(She points at his shirt, where he has spilled some food.)*

BORIS. Blady. *[Fuck.]*

DIANA. Hold on, one minute. *(She gets some seltzer and a napkin.)* Let me do. Tell me, you see him before you leaving, or what?

BORIS. Who?

DIANA. Papa.

BORIS. No.

DIANA. Aie, come on, you not even saying goodbye / before —

BORIS. No, I'm not.

DIANA. Okay, whatever. I talk to him last month, he ask about you. Every time I call he ask. Listen, he so old now, he like different person, you know?

BORIS. Fignya. *[Bullshit.]*

DIANA. Is true, is like you talking to a rabbit. He don' even understand what he saying. Last time — Last time I call, we on za phone maybe half hour. I'm telling him everything what's doing, almost everything — I ask what he up to. Then I go to hang up, and he say, "Okay, Pogovorim skoro, Masha." *[Talk to you soon, Masha.]*

BORIS. Who's Masha?

DIANA. I asking za nurse, after, "Who's Masha"? She say is some old bitch he sleeping wiz from down za hall. I'm telling you, like a rabbit. Listen, za parent you want should die first never does. Never. You can be mad, you cannot be mad. Is not going to change. *(Mira enters the office.)*

MIRA. Hello?

DIANA. Okay, finally.

MIRA. Hey, where is everyone?

DIANA. You wanna party when you get home? Everyone is hiding. They gonna yell "Soo-prize!" In a minute's gonna be.

MIRA. You don't have to be a jerk about / it —

DIANA. You asking me stupid question, you get stupid answer. Where you coming from, five o'clock? School is over long time, arready.

MIRA. I was hanging out.

DIANA. Where you hanging?

MIRA. Oh my God, K.G.B. — Nowhere — I was with Ilona, we decided to walk.

DIANA. Next time you decide something, you send me a text, you call me. I have blood pressure, you understand? *(Diana exits to the kitchen.)*

MIRA. Fine. *(To Boris.)* Whoa — Hello.

BORIS. No one can get dressed in zis house, ah?

MIRA. You look like you're goin' to a funeral, or something.

BORIS. Little optimeest *[optimist]*. Is birthday party — Nobody dead, yet.

MIRA. Are you gonna get wasted?

BORIS. Totally. I'm getting like totally wasted, man.

MIRA. What is this? *(She examines his tie, as Diana reenters.)*

BORIS. It's silk.

MIRA. This is like, not your color.

BORIS. This my color, big time.

MIRA. No way — You are totally an autumn.

DIANA. Hey, you planning on doing something tonight, or you going to hang all over everyone.

MIRA. … Yeah.

BORIS. … You have cleaner you like?

DIANA. Lemme see. Just put in za wash, is gonna come out.

BORIS. Ti Oovyeryena? *[Yeah?]*

DIANA. Yeah, you have what to wear something, now?

BORIS. Da, da. *[Yeah, yeah.]*

DIANA. Okay, so I doing it later.

BORIS. Slushaye, zavtra — *[Listen, tomorrow —]*

DIANA. Ya skazala, ne volnooyecya. *[I said, don't worry.]*

BORIS. Ya znayu, naw — *[I know, but —]*

DIANA. I'm telling you, thank you, but no thank you. Let him take care of his own shit. *(Boris exits up the stairs into Mira's room to change.)*

MIRA. What's up with tomorrow?

DIANA. Mind you own business. Hey look here. *(Diana takes a pair of boots out of a bag.)* There is girl in my store — Yesterday, she buying new pair, this one she was going to throw away. Very warm, still. I think it's you size — Try.

MIRA. It smells like foot sweat.

DIANA. What you want it should smell like? Put in Lysol, 'sgonna be fine. I wanna see it fits or no. *(Mira puts on the shoes.)*

MIRA. Um, do you know where we keep the tax returns?

DIANA. Yeah.

MIRA. Well, I'm doing this project for school — For math. It's about like, managing your finances, for when you're older.

DIANA. Mm-hm.

MIRA. Yeah, they're gonna like show us how to go over it and they just want us to like bring an example of — Of what it looks like, I guess? And then we have to figure out like our, um — Tax bracket?

DIANA. Tax bracket. That's a big word.

MIRA. … Right. I thought you kept it in there.

DIANA. You know, usually when someone want you tax information, they call you.

MIRA. Oh really?

DIANA. Yeah.

MIRA. … Did they do that? … Okay, this is not even a big deal. It's basically — So, I'm technically in for the August slot, but they need your financial information, like to see if I'm eligible for aid, and that could cover everything — I mean like airfare — Everything.

DIANA. Do me a favor — End it arready —

MIRA. / Ma —

DIANA. Because let say they giving you za money, you going to cry a lot more when I say you can't go, right?

MIRA. But I don't think you would say no if I got a scholarship.

DIANA. Really?

MIRA. Yeah, I just feel like that would make you a really bad mother.

DIANA. … Walk around za office few times. Tell me if is comfortable for you. *(Mira walks back and forth in the office.)* How it feels — Good?

MIRA. It's like shaped to someone else's feet, I don't know.

DIANA. So, now is gonna shape to you feet. Is waterproof. I think is Timberland.

MIRA. They're fine. You know if you're worried, you can talk to people — They have someone you can / talk to —

DIANA. Okay, do me a favor, put away za garbage before everyone come home — Is like a wasteland you got over here.

MIRA. I just think — Maybe because you've never done it, you're nervous about me going away. Totally understandable. But if you talk to one of the instructors or something, it might just like relax you about the whole thing.

DIANA. And put za paper in recyclable. I don' need a ticket. *(Boris comes back downstairs.)* Ti sobirayeshcya pozdno veernootsa? *[You going to be home late?]*

BORIS. Yesli voobshche. *[If at all.]*

DIANA. Be quiet you coming in late.

BORIS. For sure.

MIRA. Hey, first time you left home, how old were you?

BORIS. You know, I don't — I don't remember —

MIRA. Like a teenager?

DIANA. Can you leave him alone / please?

MIRA. I'm just asking someone who's actually done this before — Who's been / someplace —

DIANA. Why you don' go upstairs you have a nice room where you can shut za door —

MIRA. No, seriously, we were talking about this the other day / and —

DIANA. About what?

MIRA. About me going to Italy —

DIANA. / What?

MIRA. You know, and I mean — He, at least, gets / it —

DIANA. What were you talking?

BORIS. / Nothing —

MIRA. Like he understands that it's normal, people do this —

DIANA. Can you please tell me what / she talking?

49

MIRA. People my age, I mean you said, right?

BORIS. I really / don't —

MIRA. He just said it's important for girls to travel.

DIANA. ... Okay listen, I see you wanna do a lot around here, but do me a favor — Don' help me and don' help her, panyamayesh? *[Understand?]*

BORIS. ... Except when you ask me, right?

DIANA. Exactly. That's what I get for giving you a bed, food and hot water.

BORIS. See, I thinking maybe you confused.

DIANA. I'm not.

BORIS. Yeah, I think you are, because last time I see you I was eighteen, so maybe in you mind, I don't know — I'm still eighteen, but I'm not, so do me a favor and watch you mouth when you talk to me.

DIANA. *(To Mira.)* ... Give me za shoes, I'm gonna spray. And make za bed, I don' like looking at zis when we eating.

MIRA. Ma, this is really important — Like life important, Boris was just — I mean he was just saying what a good idea it was, right?

DIANA. *(To Boris.)* You know, few weeks ago, this one not coming home lying to my face. So excuse me, if I have little problem wiz whatever going / on.

MIRA. What's going on — The fact that someone in this house actually agrees with / me?

DIANA. She don't understand you, but I do, okay? And I don' like it.

BORIS. Te eta serosnaya? *[Seriously?]*

DIANA. You talk to her little bit and all of a sudden she lying all the way home.

MIRA. Oh my God, how am I lying?

BORIS. I don't know what you / meaning —

DIANA. You don't?

BORIS. No.

DIANA. Look at me.

BORIS. Come on.

MIRA. Stop it.

DIANA. Look at me.

MIRA. Ma, what is your problem?

BORIS. You ever think maybe is not question of what I'm saying, what I'm doing?

DIANA. No.

BORIS. Ask her where she coming from right now — Right now.

Mira, is taking you so long to walk home from school? In December, is taking you so long?

MIRA. … Yes.

BORIS. So if Mama call you friend right now, she gonna tell her same thing?

MIRA. What are you doing?

BORIS. Or maybe instead, you meeting za boys after school, doing what you do and coming home and lying.

MIRA. I'm not — I mean, it's nothing —

DIANA. What?!

MIRA. It's nothing!

DIANA. Mira —

MIRA. Okay, fine, there's a guy, and … And sometimes we walk home, / that's it —

DIANA. What guy?

MIRA. No / one.

DIANA. What you doing with no one for two hours?

MIRA. Just — Talking!

DIANA. I know what that means when you fourteen!

MIRA. *(To Boris.)* What the / hell?

BORIS. I'm not making her do anything, she not doing arready. And by za way, I'm not you son, I'm not you husband, okay? Don' forget. *(He exits.)*

DIANA. You better start talking. *(Blackout. Transition: Late at night. Mira is asleep on the air mattress. Alex enters through the office, careful not to wake her. He takes some money from his wallet and puts it in the envelope atop the wall unit. He looks at Mira. He exits upstairs.)*

Scene 3

The office. Mira sits at the desk, while Misha looks over her shoulder. His face is healed.

MISHA. This is accounts payable.

MIRA. I'm doing it arready, no? I'll ask you if I need —

MISHA. I help — No, this is help —

MIRA. It's not if I don't need it —

MISHA. / Arright —

MIRA. Then it's just ann-oying.

MISHA. So go. I'm quiet. *(Mira works for a moment.)* Very good.

MIRA. It's not so hard — A monkey could do it.

MISHA. No-no — After only a week, you knowing? Smart, you number smart. Last girl, she not so good like you. She having a baby now — A boy, you know Yeva?

MIRA. No.

MISHA. Nice girl. Is taking her long time to have za baby — She doing za in-vee-tero. Listen, when you finish we go downstairs — Zev having to leave early — I need you on dispatch.

MIRA. What?

MISHA. Don' worry. Za radio very easy to use — And they is price list, is gonna show you how much to charge.

MIRA. Why can't you do it?

MISHA. I got pickup in Bay Ridge. What za difference, you sitting up here, you sitting down there?

MIRA. The drivers. No, seriously they're always like hanging around, and the big one, you know —

MISHA. Igor —

MIRA. I don't know, really big — Like really —

MISHA. Yeah, Igor —

MIRA. Well, last time I was down there, he went to the bathroom and he like — He didn't close the door all the way.

MISHA. So if he do again, tell him close it!

MIRA. I can't do that when he's like mid-pee, come on.

MISHA. Look, I don' have anyone for dispatch — I can't have za phone just ringing, you understand?

MIRA. This is bullshit.

MISHA. You not za first one who eat bullshit, you not gonna be za last. Ah, look okay — When you getting credit card receipt, you put in za file cabinet, what's here — Hold on. If someone call, they wanting a copy we can send, arright? Is taking little bit time, but you tell them we can fax — I got za printer what's also a fax machine. *(Alex enters.)*

ALEX. What-up?

MISHA. Hey, arright — Now we in business. Tell you sister is not so hard to run dispatch, she crying her eyes off.

MIRA. I'm not / crying —

MISHA. All she having to do is sit in za window and pick up a phone.

ALEX. What's up with Zev?

MISHA. Uch, his mother she got cancer.

ALEX. / Jeez —

MISHA. Yeah, liver. She should live a hundred year, but I'm telling you — She picked absolute worst time for chemo. Za holiday? Come on — Now is picking up, and I having to worry she gonna die — Boom — Seven days shiva. Who I'm gonna find to sit down there?

MIRA. Why don't you just pull me out of school, put me on salary —

MISHA. Hey, you don't like being here, next time walk home from school little bit faster. Ah, fuck — Is all in wrong order — People just sticking in like we never gonna find! *(Alex sits and separates money from an envelope.)* Take off you coat, you gonna overheat youself —

ALEX. I'm fine.

MISHA. You getting fives?

ALEX. Hold on, lemme count it out.

MISHA. Arright. You can drive maybe until ten o'clock, tonight? I only got six guys on.

ALEX. Oh, I wish you would've told me. I picked up a shift at the store.

MISHA. How many days you at Verizon this week?

ALEX. Like four, I guess.

MISHA. What za fuck?

ALEX. It's Christmas.

MISHA. So what? For me is also Christmas, no?

ALEX. Well, they're doing a little better so —

MISHA. Excuse me?

ALEX. I just mean… They need me — I can make more there, so it's like more worth it, you know? For everybody.

MISHA. … Yeah, sure, I know. So you driving anything for me, tonight?

ALEX. I guess I could do an hour or two, but then I should really get there.

MISHA. … How is going wiz invoices?

MIRA. It's thrilling — I'm really finding myself. *(They all work.)*

ALEX. Ma said direct deposit went through, arready — Like for mortgage?

MISHA. Is fifteenth.

ALEX. Yeah. Well, I gave her maybe half — The rest I think was from her bakery, but um — I just didn't know if she had anything left over to give you for your ... you know, expenses or whatever.

MISHA. Don' worry.

ALEX. Nah, I'm not worried, it's just — The store's been slammed, so — I mean, I got there Tuesday, there was a line out the door, like to Beverly. And it was only four o'clock — Sick. And it stayed like that 'til closing.

MISHA. Interesting tale what you weaving for us.

ALEX. Pop. If you need something — Like to tide you over ... You should lemme know.

MISHA. ... Something like what?

ALEX. I don't know — Whatever. Couple of hundred.

MISHA. ... Yeah?

ALEX. Sure, it's been like I said, so ... I mean, how much you / need?

MISHA. Lemme look at few things and I tell you.

ALEX. Arright ... I'm gonna drop this at the bank and then, I guess I'll just — I don't know — I'll drive 'til five, five-thirty?

MISHA. And then you going to za store —

ALEX. Uh-huh —

MISHA. Hey hold one second for me. *(To Mira.)* Good, just add up — There is calculator. Alex, eh last week I was thinking you was supposed to do dispatch on Saturday night.

ALEX. Oh —

MISHA. But when I coming home Robert was doing.

ALEX. Yeah, I don't even ... God what was Saturday night — I think I was like — You know honestly, I might have just been hangin' out. I'm sorry, yeah I was just wrecked from the week.

MISHA. Okay, no problem. Question number two: How you have extra couple hundred dollars sitting around?

ALEX. What?

MISHA. I know my wife.

ALEX. I told you, it's been busy.

MISHA. Yeah, but is not cash business, Verizon. She seeing what you making. You telling me she give you a bonus, or something?

ALEX. ... Look, I'm just trying to help you out, but if you feel weird about it, I totally understand. Forget it.

MISHA. This is almost like an answer, except for za fact that it's nothing like an answer —

ALEX. Jesus —

MISHA. So why don' you tell me how you can be so generous, all of a sudden.

ALEX. ... Come on. It's nothin', I been picking up a little extra work —

MISHA. What kind of / work?

ALEX. Just around — I been finding / stuff —

MISHA. Where you / finding —

ALEX. Nowhere —

MISHA. From where / you —

ALEX. From Boris, okay? It's nothing — He — He had some — Like errands, I could help him out with, and with everything going on with you it's like, right time, right place, you know?

MIRA. What are you, getting coffee for him?

ALEX. No, I'm just ... No.

MISHA. How long?

ALEX. Not that long —

MISHA. How long!

ALEX. A couple of weeks.

MISHA. ... You fucking mother. Arright, a couple of weeks, so few hundred dollars.

ALEX. Pretty much.

MISHA. So hey, now is a lot of sales, why you don' go buy something? Go buy something — Maybe you need 'lectronics, maybe you want some new jeans, I don' know, but now you having little bit in you pocket, so maybe start looking around.

ALEX. But I know you could use it.

MISHA. If you can't spend za money, what make you think I can? *(The phone rings.)* Yeah, we coming — *(To Mira.)* Go start on dispatch. Zev have to leave. *(She goes towards the house.)* Where you going?

MIRA. I wanna use our bathroom. *(She exits, stands in the house and listens.)*

MISHA. Okay, get out. You fired. You don' got no 1099's here no more, so you can leave or I call security is gonna walk you out.

ALEX. This is ridiculous —

MISHA. What you mad 'bout? Lot of people losing they job — They don't got nothing to be falling back on. You — you have long career as a piece of shit coming you way. What you doing for him? Don't tell me, forget — Okay, what you doing?

ALEX. Nothing —

MISHA. You driving, you inside, you what?

ALEX. What do you mean inside?

MISHA. I mean, I wanna know if you ever touched one.

ALEX. One what?

MISHA. A girl! I wanna know if you ever touched one.

ALEX. … I really don't know what you're talking about —

MISHA. Don't bullshit me!

ALEX. I'm not! Arright, it's a couple of nights a week for him, that's it. And all I do — Seriously, all I do, is I go to the pier — In Midtown. Pier 52. They gotta bunch of shit, you know, like alligator shirts, DVDs — Stolen, right? And they give me a truck for the night. I drop it all off in Chinatown and that's it, I swear. Look, I'm not … I'm not doing anything you have to like — Be that way about.

MISHA. You think I know someone for twenty years, and who they are is like Magical Mystery —

ALEX. Maybe it is, 'cause I don't / even —

MISHA. You stealing Gucci bags for him —

ALEX. Yes, and you know what — sidebar — Who are you borrowing money from, 'cause it doesn't look like small business loan, you know what I'm sayin'?

MISHA. Anton? Oh my God, he a nothing, Alex. Yeah, he think he big, but everything what he give me, I know where is coming from. He running za gamble in back of Vasily's. He getting money from za shops on Beach Avenue — That's it.

ALEX. Well how's that any different from this?

MISHA. How is … Okay, tell me again where you going tonight.

ALEX. To work.

MISHA. At za store?

ALEX. Yes. *(Misha walks up, gets close him and feels his jacket.)* I am. What are you doing — get off — *(Misha finds a gun.)*

MISHA. Fuck.

ALEX. That's for just in case.

MISHA. In case what — A DVD runs away? … Three weeks? Three weeks and you bringing a gun into my house?

ALEX. I'm not in the house. *(Misha puts the gun on the table. He gets his coat.)*

MISHA. … I having pickup in Bay Ridge, some asshole — Italian guy who he like only a Lincoln, no Cadillac. Fucking preferences. … Shit, you know — I remember when you was — When I was stealing you from za hospital in Russia. Over there they hanging babies from za ceiling like King Tut — So tight they not moving, and they not letting za father inside — You can believe? But, I take you. You was ... You was little baby for tiny coffin, little jaundice baby, but I take you anyway because fuck za hospital, fuck za nurses what they say, "You still young — You can have more." This my son. He still alive — He gonna stay alive. And we taking you to Hungarian doctor and he feed you bright light and you live. And I wish ... I wish I would keep za receipt, because I looking at you right now and I swear to God, I would return you for store credit.

ALEX. Listen / I —

MISHA. Do me a favor, go pack youself a suitcase — When I come back I don't want you here.

ALEX. / Wait —

MISHA. And if I see you 'round my house 'sgonna be big problems, you hear me? I'm knowing Tommy from down za street, he FDNY, he knowing a lot of cops.

ALEX. Pop, wait —

MISHA. Mira! *(He opens the door.)* Nu come on, davai. *[Let's go.]*

MIRA. Alex, you can get in big trouble for that stuff —

MISHA. Let's go —

MIRA. Really, like major trouble —

MISHA. Now! *(She exits out the office.)*

ALEX. Pop, listen — You don't have to do this. It's a couple of hundred bucks, I swear I'm not even — *(Misha slams the door. After a moment, Alex gets the gun and exits.)*

Scene 4

Mira's room. Mira packs Boris' things. Boris enters from the front door. He checks around the house.

BORIS. Alex? ... Alex? *(Boris enters the bedroom.)*

MIRA. I want my room back.

BORIS. This is not a problem —

MIRA. Good, so get out.

BORIS. Where's you brother?

MIRA. I don't know.

BORIS. Listen, I move everything downstairs / tonight —

MIRA. You're not gonna be / downstairs —

BORIS. Right now, tell me where I can find / Alex —

MIRA. You're not gonna be downstairs, and I don't know where he is. Pop kicked him out.

BORIS. ... Why he do that?

MIRA. I guess he got mad when he found out you guys were bartending together.

BORIS. Today, they talking?

MIRA. Yeah.

BORIS. Okay. Look Mira, I don't tell you everything 'bout myself, only because is very confidential work what I do —

MIRA. / Please —

BORIS. In fact I sign contract so legally, I cannot release information.

MIRA. Oh, you a lawyer or something — Like a C.I.A. operative-Boris-and-Natasha-bullshit?

BORIS. Exactly like this.

MIRA. I know, okay.

BORIS. ... What you know?

MIRA. What you're doing. I know, Alex told us. *(He closes the door.)* Whatayou gonna offer me a summer internship?

BORIS. Okay, we talk now, yeah?

MIRA. I don't need to talk / to you —

BORIS. You are angry with me, I know —

MIRA. What?

BORIS. What I say to Mama, 'bout you boyfriend —

MIRA. This isn't even about / that —

BORIS. Maybe you don' get to go / away —

MIRA. I totally will — God, you are like not that important.

BORIS. Then why you so mad?

MIRA. ... You should get out of here before my dad gets home.

BORIS. Listen, you brother gonna be in big trouble if you are talking to people.

MIRA. Oh yeah?

BORIS. Big trouble.

MIRA. But maybe not so much. I mean, like maybe if he gets caught, which I'm sure he totally will, then they'll wanna know who he's working for. It's not like in Russia, you know?

BORIS. … What, you making me promises? Promises you are making to me? Like you don't do anything, like you not thinking disgusting / things —

MIRA. Whatayou talking about?

BORIS. In school you having private boyfriend. At home, you kissing me?

MIRA. That was a mistake —

BORIS. Mistake or secret? Mistake is always secret, yes? But secret is not always mistake. You still seeing you boyfriend?

MIRA. He's not my boyfriend.

BORIS. Yeah, I know — It's complicated. *(She goes to leave. He grabs her arm, and holds her close.)*

MIRA. Whatayou doing?

BORIS. Whatchu want me to do?

MIRA. Leave. Like, move-out-of-here-leave. *(He covers her mouth.)*

BORIS. I am not lawyer. Also, I am not C.I.A. You know why? I don't like when people fuck with me. You know what's this? "Fuck With"? In my home, everybody fuck with you. To police, you give money, also to judge. Everybody you give a little something. So whatchu want? To stay quiet — You want money? No? *(He tries to kiss her, but she turns away.)* No? *(He pushes her back on the bed.)* You know what happen when a little girl try to fuck with you? She is easy to take care of. *(He puts his hand down her pants. It's a violent and sudden gesture.)*

ALEX. *(Offstage.)* Hello?

MIRA. Stop it!

BORIS. You understand?

MIRA. Please! *(Boris and Mira sit up as Alex opens the door.)*

ALEX. Mira?

BORIS. Come in, come in.

ALEX. What's up, I heard —

BORIS. What you hear? Si' down, pashalasta. *[Please]* Sit. You wanna pillow? You missed important appointment today.

ALEX. I know, I / got —

BORIS. And now you sister tell me she knowing what work you do for me. So it sound like you did some major fucking up this afternoon.

ALEX. Listen, I didn't — she doesn't like, know know —

MIRA. Alex —

ALEX. Shut-up.

BORIS. Because, we have problem if you got big mouth.

ALEX. I know. I didn't … I mean I …

BORIS. Yeah, yeah, go, I listen.

ALEX. Pop was on my case, so I told him, you know, about like stereos and pocketbooks and — Like moving shit, or whatever.

BORIS. Ah. Okay.

ALEX. So it's no big deal.

MIRA. Alex, whatayou —

ALEX. Shut the fuck up.

BORIS. Shh-shh-shh. It's okay, it's okay. So what I'm gonna say if there is question?

ALEX. There won't be.

BORIS. Yeah? But in pretend sit-uation, let say a police gonna call me, he heard something —

ALEX. She's not gonna say anything.

BORIS. Oh. For sure?

ALEX. I promise.

BORIS. You also promise?

ALEX. Come on, she won't say anything. I swear.

BORIS. *(To Mira.)* Hey.

MIRA. I promise.

ALEX. Get out of here.

MIRA. Ca' I talk to you for a minute?

ALEX. Get out! *(She exits.)*

BORIS. Okay, second order business. You know this word, competency? In America, government is competency, yes? Workers is competency? Alex, tell me why I had a girl standing in passenger pickup today, when instead she should be in you car.

ALEX. … Listen, my dad's gonna be here soon, and I'm supposed to —

BORIS. What we are discussing? We are talking work or we are talking family?

ALEX. I'm just saying, he's gonna flip out if he sees me.

BORIS. You scared from him?

ALEX. No.

BORIS. Good. He loud, but he a pussy —

ALEX. He's not —

BORIS. From him you don't have to be scared.

ALEX. My dad's not… a pussy —

BORIS. Okay, I don't give one shit-or-two 'bout you father. Only

60

thing I care 'bout is I had one more girl today and one less car.

ALEX. I was on my way to JFK, and I … I just couldn't. And I knew I had to come back here and pack and I shoulda sent you a text or something but I didn't — I just …

BORIS. That's it?

ALEX. Yeah?

BORIS. You think this is — Like a class, what you not showing up for? Ah? What I'm supposed to tell my guy, when he got a scared little bitch asking him questions for twenty minutes before he can find ride for her?

ALEX. I don't know.

BORIS. Think.

ALEX. … Can I have a cigarette?

BORIS. … Yeah, you can have a cigarette. *(Boris lights two cigarettes and gives one to Alex.)* You know, when you just start, in za beginning? Is hard for everyone. I see you father when he start, pshh. You ever see a man much older than you crying?

ALEX. I'm not Mira — You can't just, like, make shit up, okay.

BORIS. Serious. He never tell you, ah? I'm not suprizing. You ever hear Tomsk?

ALEX. What?

BORIS. Tomsk.

ALEX. I don't know what that is.

BORIS. Ah, it's beautiful. Beautiful place, wiz the Universities. Is like — Cambridge, England. Like Russian Cambridge, very nice. Zis is where we meet.

ALEX. Okay, see? I know you're both from Smolensk.

BORIS. I know him little bit from where I grow up, is fact. But always, I am considering Tomsk our, like, eh — Introduction. What he tell you, we meet when they get married? Some bullshit, he tell you?

ALEX. You did.

BORIS. You ever think is strange how he knowing everything, Misha. What, he Rasputin or something? Answer not so complicate. He knowing because he doing. Listen, in Russia we are moving girls and one stop is Tomsk. Zis was bad time, Yeltsin time, nobody got shit. Eh, wiz Soviets also nobody got shit, but now you can talk about how you don' have shit. So in Tomsk, we have stop for za' girls where we are doing … Job training. And I am working in the house. I do inventory — Like you, wiz Verizon. Anyway, one

61

day we get new driver — You Poppa. And he come inside wiz za girl. You know why? No? Oldest reason. He is having to use toilet. And Victor — Hey, you ever talk to Victor when you are in New Jersey? No? Ah, he is like joker, like funny guy. So he say to you Poppa he do such a good job driving zis girl, he get to go first. Wiz za' girl. Always you want to go first, believe me. And Poppa he is saying "No, no thank you," But Victor, He never ask you, he tell. And now Poppa know he is stupid for not holding it. He should wait next time and go into cafe, by a tree is better than to come in za house. But what he gonna do? Zis is good job, for Yeltsin time. So whachu think happen?

ALEX. I don't know.

BORIS. No? Okay, you ever want to be wiz girl, but you — Like you nervous? Nothing going on, nothing coming up, right? And now Poppa he saying, "I am only driver — Please — I only want to drive." And za girl is crying of course, and I'm saying, "Asshole, come on, leave him alone." But when Victor having a fun time, you can' tell him to stop. So he hold a gun up to Poppa, who now is crying like baby and — You know what happen? He hold it for so long, he can't hold it no more — He yeah, he go on himself. So now there is piss all over him, his clothes, za girl. And Victor, he just laugh and laugh … First few job is hard, Alex — I know. But only once I'm telling you: You fuck up big time when you mess wiz merchandise. You making trouble for me, for a lotta guys, you understand? You big time Fuck-upsky. When they is guy standing in front of police waiting for you ass, I got problem. And when I got problem, you got problem. So, here what we gonna say. You was driving to airport and you getting za ticket. And officer, he writing down you plate number and he look at you little bit funny, like he smell something. And you start driving and then you see he following you from za back.

ALEX. Okay —

BORIS. Shut-up. So you thinking — I can' go to airport, because he gonna know — He gonna see everything, za policeman. So instead you driving 'round, maybe half hour, and you doing everyone a big favor, because you a sharp guy. Who forget to charge his fucking phone.

ALEX. I'm really sorry.

BORIS. Ach. Zatknees. *[Shut up.]* This is not a Russian sentiment: Sorry. You did it, it's done. Pizdyetz. *[It's over.]*

ALEX. … I could like, maybe get you some free phones or something. … You're going?

BORIS. Yeah, I don' need to listen to an asshole yell at me for two hours, tonight. This is benefit of being grown man. Hey you want zis? *(He holds up a tie.)* I'm buying, but now I don' think is my color. Okay, rest of zis shit, you bring me tomorrow.

ALEX. Okay.

BORIS. … You making a headache for me, Alex.

ALEX. Well maybe I'm just not-like-cut out or whatever.

BORIS. Maybe. We gonna see.

ALEX. Whatayou mean?

BORIS. You got pickup in two hour — Newark. Delta Terminal. Only now, you doing some work which is gratis. You know gratis? Is U-O-ME. Like I-O-U is for you. This is U-O-ME.

ALEX. But —

BORIS. Nye boody durakom. *[Don't be stupid.]* You know what I never tell you? I am also little bit like joker, like a funny guy. You call me tonight, you understand? *(Alex nods. Boris exits with a duffel bag.)*

Scene 5

Mira is in the office. Diana enters having just come from work.

DIANA. Whachu alone? What happening wiz Poppa?

MIRA. He got a late call.

DIANA. Okay so come on, I'm home — You can be finish in here. You wan' help me to start dinner? Nu, come on.

MIRA. I'm not hungry.

DIANA. Hey, guess who I see today. I see Zhanna — You remember her from the junior high? She working in House of Jeans — She selling jean-sweatshirt, you know this? … You having a day, so you having a day. *(Diana enters the living room.)* Hey is late, so maybe let's order a pizza!

MIRA. I told you, I'm not hungry!

DIANA. If you want better, Chinese food, we could get — *(Alex enters from upstairs, with an overnight bag. To Alex.)* Hey, I call, you don' answer today? Whatchu got za briefcase for? … *(Mira enters living room.)* What we got, deaf and dumb here?

ALEX. Um …

MIRA. Pop kicked him out.

DIANA. … Go put away za bag. We ordering Chinese.

ALEX. Listen, I'm just gonna stay with Eugene tonight —

DIANA. I don' think so —

ALEX. I arready called him, it's / fine —

DIANA. Zatknees. *[Shut up.]* If I wanna hear you voice, I let you know. Awn boodyet gavareet smayeem sinam? *[He's gonna talk to my son?]* He don' even call — He don' even ask me? I don' think so. *(To Mira.)* You. Get za menu for za Chinese! Instead he sending you to Eugene. To stay wiz a Latvian? No, no, no. You know when he get to make rules in zis place? When he get to decide? When I got worms crawling 'round in my eye socket, you get me? *(To Mira.)* Good — Circle sweet and sour shrimp!

MIRA. Large or small?

DIANA. Large! Boodyet re-shayt v'mayom daw-me? Ya nye dumay-oo. *[Gonna decide in my house? I don't think so.]* What else you want? What else!

MIRA. I don' / want —

DIANA. Give to me. *(Diana exits to the kitchen.)*

ALEX. Are you okay?

MIRA. What are you really doing for Boris? *(Diana enters with a cordless phone.)*

DIANA. Go unpack za' briefcase.

ALEX. Ma —

DIANA. If you think even for one night you gonna sleep away from this house, you more stupid than I'm thinking.

ALEX. I'm not stupid!

DIANA. … Si' down. *(Misha enters.)*

MISHA. You order arready?

DIANA. Lemme ask you a question. You think is okay you kick my son out of my house — You don' even maybe ask me first?

MISHA. Yeah, I think is okay.

DIANA. Do me a favor don't —

MISHA. No! No more favor for you — I doing you one favor, look what happening —

DIANA. Listen, you don' like what is going on here, you can go sleep in you car, tonight. In you office — I get za sleeping bag for you, right now! *(Misha picks up the cordless phone and dials.)*

MISHA. I told you I not joking wiz you.

ALEX. I know.

MISHA. *(On the phone.)* Yeah, hello — Okay, I wan' delivery.

DIANA. Bo zhemoy — *[My God —]*

MISHA. 2320 East 23rd Street — Upstairs. Between W and X — Okay, one order pork dumplings … Eh, steam — please. Large sweet and sour shrimp, large chicken lo mein, large egg drop soup, also few spring roll — Mira, you wan' spring roll? *(She shakes her head.)* So, just one spring roll and give me za … No, that's it. How long? Ah-ha, how much? Okay. *(He hangs up.)* Twenty minutes is coming — If you still here, big trouble 'gonna be. *(To Diana.)* You know he give him a gun, you brother? Yeah, you know everything. Big time Soviet operative this one. You know what is happen to za Soviet operative, Mirachka? 'Lectic chair. Zzzt. Like a barbeque 'gonna be. I'm buying ketchup and beets to put on you Mama. You ever put beets on a hamburger?

DIANA. Don' talk to her, such things.

MISHA. Why, no? She my business partner. You take one from me, I take one from you. Is even, no?

DIANA. You see — He jealous somebody finally making some money.

MISHA. You believe zis shit? You mother rip up you insides! Is poison like Clorox. You drink up good, Alex — Drink up!

DIANA. Yeah, he mad his son gotta come save him from his stupid.

MISHA. My stupid?

DIANA. / Yeah —

MISHA. Whachu talking my stupid?

DIANA. This one get's the money — He don' also gotta have the stitches!

MISHA. Ach, you so fucked up.

DIANA. What "fucked up?" Providing for you family? Zis is how you call "fucked up"?

MISHA. This what you wan' call it now?

DIANA. To take money for working zis is "fucked up"? To put a dinner on you table — Is nothing to be shame from, believe / you me —

MISHA. For you, no.

DIANA. So you give a girl a ride! … A stupid girl. She so smart, she don't end up in you car, no? She so smart, she go to college — She don't go looking, am I right?

MIRA. ... What girl?

DIANA. Listen, Mira. Here is important thing to know, okay? Most important. We arready got problems in zis house. We don't need nobody else's.

MISHA. No. No, tell her. Come on, you also — Doing a lot what you can' even say. Everything I do, I can say, you understand?

DIANA. Ya mogu skazat, shtaw ti — *[I can say what you do —]*

MISHA. Everything! Tomorrow, I working in Tommy garage, so he give me za free oil change. You know what I do for him? I mop his office, clean his toilet. I should be 'shame from zis?

DIANA. To scrub a toilet for an oil change? Yeah, at least if you scrub a toilet, bring home a steak! *(Diana touches Alex.)*

ALEX. Don't touch me. You don't even —

DIANA. What —

ALEX. ASK! You don't even fuckin' ASK ME?

DIANA. Why I should ask? You know, I don't see is such big problem for you.

ALEX. Because you decided it wasn't?

DIANA. No, because I notice you not stopping. You know everything a long time arready, but still you doing it. God, everybody in zis house hate za medicine. Of course. Medicine tastes like shit! But you take anyway, right? I take, you take — Everybody! Now you gonna walk in here like all of a sudden you too good for it? After you doing for how long? Alex, you don' have no legs you standing on. And you don' have to go out from zis house, right now. Not because he say so.

ALEX. Yeah, I do actually. I gotta go to work.

MISHA. No, no, no — You don' gotta do shit — You choosing / it.

ALEX. Oh, come / on —

MISHA. You want to!

ALEX. Bull! Shit! You tellin' me you wake up in the morning and get in your car because you want to? Takin' a piss in a bottle, 'cause you can't afford the fuckin' ticket for double parking, because you want to? Fuckin' comin' home talking 'bout this asshole tellin' you what radio station he wants, this asshole tellin' you how he wants you to drive. You're actually gonna stand there and tell me your job don't make you feel like a fuckin' loser? ... But you do it anyway. So my job ... *(Alex takes money from his wallet.)* My job makes me feel like some disgusting piece of — *(He grabs Diana's hand and gives her the cash.)* But bottom line — What's the difference? What is the difference — It's all just a way to make ends meet. It's all ... It's all the same thing. *(Alex exits.)*

MIRA. ... What girl?

DIANA. Nobody.

MIRA. Pop?

MISHA. ... Nobody? You brother, and you uncle ... And you mother.

DIANA. Stop.

MISHA. Take some girl —

DIANA. Misha.

MISHA. And make her some big promises —

DIANA. / Please.

MISHA. And steal her away from her family —

DIANA. / Don't —

MISHA. From her home —

DIANA. Don't do this.

MISHA. And all of a sudden, in one minute is over.

MIRA. ... What's over?

MISHA. ... Her life. *(He snaps his finger, music comes on and the lights shift.)*

Scene 6

The car.

SVETA. Me'nya zovut Sveta. A oni skazhali tyebe? ... K'ak tyebya zavut? *[My name is Sveta. Did they tell you that? ... What's your name?]*

ALEX. Sasha.

SVETA. Ah, Sasha? Dobriy vyecher. Eh, k'ak dolga yeshaw yehat? *[Ah, Sasha? Good evening. Eh, you know how long 'til we get there?]*

ALEX. Nemnyoga dolshe. *[A little longer.]*

SVETA. Ah-ha — Dyesyat minoot? Dvadtsat? *[Ah-ha — Ten minutes? Twenty?]* *(He turns up the radio.)* Ti n'ye dolzhen b'yit grub sa mnoiy. Ti je amerikanyits? *[You don't have to be rude. You're American, right?]*

ALEX. Ya nye amerikanyits. *[I'm not American.]*

SVETA. Ah, nyet? Taw otkuda ti? *[Oh, no? So where are you from?]*

ALEX. Zdyelai odolzheniye, zatknees! *[Do me a favor, shut up!]*

SVETA. Zatknees? Ti seriosna? *[Shut up? Are you serious?]* *(She looks out the window, and points.)* Shtaw eta za z'daniye? … Ladno, m'nye nuzhna ostanovit'sya na minutu. *[What's that building? … Okay, I need to stop for a minute.]*

ALEX. Ya skazal booyt spokoinoi, tak? *[I asked you to be quiet, right?]*

SVETA. Ladno, m'nye nuzhna ostanovit'sya na minutu — Seriozna, mne nado v'too-alet. Horoshaw, znayesh shtaw — *[I need to stop for a minute! Seriously, I have to go to toilet! Okay, you know what?]* *(She tries the door.)*

ALEX. Hey — Stop it — Get your fuckin' hands off my door! Nye trogai — *[Don't touch that!]*

SVETA. … Eezvyenee. *[I'm sorry.]*

ALEX. Prosto dyerzji rooki pre syebye. *[Just keeps your hands to yourself.]*

SVETA. … Ya dumayu shtaw bila oshibka. *[… I think there's been a mistake.]* Okay. Eh … Not right, not right. Automobile, eh — Not right. *(She mimes turning the wheel around, and going back.)* Yeah? Okay?

ALEX. Oh my God —

SVETA. Pozhalusta, vipoostye myenya. *[Please let me out.]*

ALEX. I can't.

SVETA. Ya hochu vernutseya v'aeroport! *[I want to go back to airport!]*

ALEX. I told you, I can't!

SVETA. Pazhalasta, ya hachoo! *[Please, I want —]*

ALEX. We're almost there — Just shut the fuck up arready — Please! *(She start banging, trying to get out.)* Ostav! *[Leave it —]* *(He reaches his hand back and she screams. She starts to fight him.)* Get off! Get off a me! *(In the struggle, he elbows her in the face. She starts to cry and hold her nose.)* Oh my god — Oh my god — Oh my god —

SVETA. Ya hochu domoi. *[I want to go home.]* *(He pulls the car over.)*

ALEX. Are you okay?

SVETA. Ya hochu domoi! *[I want to go home!]* *(Alex gets out of the car.)*

ALEX. Oo b'rise! *[Get out!]*

SVETA. Nyet! *[No!]*
ALEX. Oo b'rise! *[Get out!]* *(He reaches for her and she screams.)*
Fuck. *(He takes the gun out and points it at her.)* Vidye iz mashini.
[Get out of the car.] *(She does.)*
SVETA. Ya hochu, ya hochu, ya hochu — *[I want, I want, I want —]*
ALEX. Hey! Posmotri na menya! *[Look at me.]* Look at me, it's
okay! Posmatri! *[Look —]* *(He releases the magazine and hands it to
her. He backs away, she runs off. He gets back into the car. He turns
the music off.)*

Epilogue

*Misha works in the office. Mira does her homework by the
kitchen table. Diana deflates the air mattress. She finishes
and puts it away, then stands behind Mira. She touches Mira's
head. Mira pulls away and looks at her. After a moment,
Diana goes upstairs. She enters Mira's room and lies on the
bed. Alex enters the office. Misha stops his work. Alex puts the
gun on the desk. As he walks past, Misha grabs his hand. Alex
stands there. Lights fade until they are silhouetted against a
wall of red light. Fade to black.*

End of Play

PROPERTY LIST

2 full garbage bags, with clothes
Alarm clock
Cell phones
Manila envelope
Cash
Wallet
Stella D'Oro Swiss Fudge cookies
Shot glasses
Liquor bottles
Lugggage
Dishes of food
$20 bill
Gift packages, Matryoshka dolls
Cereal, bowls, milk
Set of keys
Coat, shoes
Books
Towel
Handgun
Bills, checkbook, pen
Stamps
Drink
Groceries
Seltzer, napkin
Bag with boots
Envelope with money
Cigarettes, lighter
Necktie
Duffel bag
Overnight bag
Chinese takeout menu
Cordless phone

SOUND EFFECTS

Dogs barking, getting louder
Text message bleep
Phone ringing
Radio music

NEW PLAYS

★ **CLYBOURNE PARK by Bruce Norris.** WINNER OF THE 2011 PULITZER PRIZE AND 2012 TONY AWARD. Act One takes place in 1959 as community leaders try to stop the sale of a home to a black family. Act Two is set in the same house in the present day as the now predominantly African-American neighborhood battles to hold its ground. "Vital, sharp-witted and ferociously smart." –*NY Times*. "A theatrical treasure…Indisputably, uproariously funny." –*Entertainment Weekly*. [4M, 3W] ISBN: 978-0-8222-2697-0

★ **WATER BY THE SPOONFUL by Quiara Alegría Hudes.** WINNER OF THE 2012 PULITZER PRIZE. A Puerto Rican veteran is surrounded by the North Philadelphia demons he tried to escape in the service. "This is a very funny, warm, and yes uplifting play." –*Hartford Courant*. "The play is a combination poem, prayer and app on how to cope in an age of uncertainty, speed and chaos." –*Variety*. [4M, 3W] ISBN: 978-0-8222-2716-8

★ **RED by John Logan.** WINNER OF THE 2010 TONY AWARD. Mark Rothko has just landed the biggest commission in the history of modern art. But when his young assistant, Ken, gains the confidence to challenge him, Rothko faces the agonizing possibility that his crowning achievement could also become his undoing. "Intense and exciting." –*NY Times*. "Smart, eloquent entertainment." –*New Yorker*. [2M] ISBN: 978-0-8222-2483-9

★ **VENUS IN FUR by David Ives.** Thomas, a beleaguered playwright/director, is desperate to find an actress to play Vanda, the female lead in his adaptation of the classic sadomasochistic tale *Venus in Fur*. "Ninety minutes of good, kinky fun." –*NY Times*. "A fast-paced journey into one man's entrapment by a clever, vengeful female." –*Associated Press*. [1M, 1W] ISBN: 978-0-8222-2603-1

★ **OTHER DESERT CITIES by Jon Robin Baitz.** Brooke returns home to Palm Springs after a six-year absence and announces that she is about to publish a memoir dredging up a pivotal and tragic event in the family's history—a wound they don't want reopened. "Leaves you feeling both moved and gratifyingly sated." –*NY Times*. "A genuine pleasure." –*NY Post*. [2M, 3W] ISBN: 978-0-8222-2605-5

★ **TRIBES by Nina Raine.** Billy was born deaf into a hearing family and adapts brilliantly to his family's unconventional ways, but it's not until he meets Sylvia, a young woman on the brink of deafness, that he finally understands what it means to be understood. "A smart, lively play." –*NY Times*. "[A] bright and boldly provocative drama." –*Associated Press*. [3M, 2W] ISBN: 978-0-8222-2751-9

DRAMATISTS PLAY SERVICE, INC.
440 Park Avenue South, New York, NY 10016 212-683-8960 Fax 212-213-1539
postmaster@dramatists.com www.dramatists.com